THE
SMALL
BUSINESS
ACTION
KIT

THE SMALL BUSINESS ACTION KIT

Written by business counsellors John Rosthorn, Andrew Haldane,
Edward Blackwell and John Wholey; edited by Arthur Dicken,
Bill Hood, Arthur Mottershead and John Rosthorn, all at
Macclesfield Business Ventures.

Kogan
Page

The Small Business Action Kit was written primarily by MBV's
business counsellors John Rosthorn, Andrew Haldane, Edward
Blackwell and John Wholey. It was edited by MBV's Chairman,
Secretary, Treasurer and Director respectively: Arthur Dicken of
ICI Pharmaceuticals Division, Bill Hood of William Hood & Co,
solicitors, Arthur Mottershead of Josolyne & Co, chartered
accountants, and John Rosthorn of ICI Pharmaceuticals Division.
The Editorial Committee would like to acknowledge the generous
help provided by MBV sponsors and many friends who have
contributed material included in the text. The advice and
financial help provided by a sister agency — Business Link at
Halton — have been much appreciated.

First published in Great Britain in 1986
by Kogan Page Ltd, 120 Pentonville Road, London N1 9JN
Reprinted 1986

British Library Cataloguing in Publication Data
The Small business action kit.
   1. Small business — Great Britain — Management
   I. Rosthorn, John   II. Dicken, Arthur
   658'.022'0941   HD62.7
   ISBN 1-85091-089-8

Printed and bound in Great Britain by
Dotesios (Printers) Limited, Bradford-on-Avon, Wiltshire

Contents

5. Now I Need the Cash . . .   57

6. . . . and Premises   72

7. Legal and Tax Matters   80

Macclesfield Business Ventures (MBV) was set up as a local enterprise agency in 1983. It is sponsored in cash and in kind by the following:

Shell UK
National Westminster Bank plc
Macclesfield Borough Council
Cheshire County Council
Imperial Chemical Industries plc
William Hood & Co
Josolyne & Co
R Cressy & Sons Ltd
Lightnin Mixers
Barclays Bank plc
N & M Edwards
Marks & Spencer plc
Jeffery Trading Co Ltd
Robert Jordan & Partners
Esso Petroleum Co Ltd
Umbro International Ltd
Macclesfield Trades Council
Binder Hamlyn
Macclesfield College of Further Education
H Heywood & Co
Inheritance Furniture Ltd
Bank of England
Department of Trade & Industry
National Nuclear Corporation Ltd
Gradus Limited
SISIS Equipment (Macclesfield) Ltd
Cheshire Building Society
Daniel, Ashworth & Booth
British Railways Board
Sillavan Industries
Lloyds Bank plc
Lancashire & Cheshire County Newspapers Ltd
IPAM (Investment Planning Analysis & Management)
Willow Group
Citibank NA
John Siddall & Sons
British Aerospace plc
Ciba-Geigy plc
Richmond Press Ltd
Midland Bank plc
Macclesfield District Federation of Commerce and Industry

MBV exists to help the generation of business growth in small businesses in the Borough of Macclesfield. Its address is Venture House, Cross Street, Macclesfield, Cheshire SK11 7PG.

Foreword

by David Trippier, RD, JP, MP, Parliamentary Under-Secretary
of State for Trade and Industry

Setting up in business, or expanding an existing small business, is an exciting experience and one which can bring high rewards. But such steps are often dangerous ones to take as the business failure rates show. As many as one-third of start-ups fail in the first year, and four-fifths have failed in five years.

Thus I welcome this Business Kit as a means by which small businesses can be helped to grow and expand in a sound way. The kit will, I believe, find good use among local enterprise agencies — the development of which I have been delighted to support. In addition, I expect that business counsellors in the Small Firms Service, the clearing banks, and accountancy practices, will want to use the kit.

As a nation we need more entrepreneurship, and I would like this kit to contribute to the establishment of new and skilled entrepreneurs.

Introduction

Fifteen hundred business counselling interviews have provided
the information on which this book is based. The explanations,
summaries and specimen work sheets are designed for use by
business counsellors, ranging from those in the professions to
those involved in voluntary counselling. The content is arranged
to meet the specific needs of business clients labouring under a
problem or with an opportunity; it will provide useful leads for
counsellors and their clients who will probably need professional
assistance in order to reap the greatest benefit from the material.
Ideally, each new start-up should have its own copy and use it
as a guide, designing its own work sheets from the examples
provided.

Every endeavour has been made to ensure accuracy at the time
of going to press, but readers are reminded that new legislation
is passed and regulations changed through the daily activities
of Parliament.

John Rosthorn

Am I Up to Running My Own Business?

Introduction

For most adults, there are but three options: unemployment, employment and self-employment. Please write down the advantages and disadvantages of each in your own circumstances.

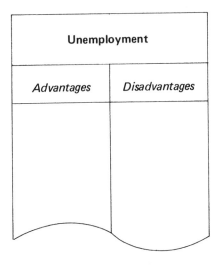

This book is mainly concerned with the successful establishment and expansion of self-employment which will in turn provide employment opportunities for others.

Ideas for business

While there are a small number of 'ideas' magazines and consultants around, most would-be businessmen have to work it out for themselves.

Business ideas may be generated through two routes:

1. Inspirational

- A gap in the market-place not satisfied by existing suppliers.
- A new solution to an existing problem; an invention, a process or method.

2. Analytical

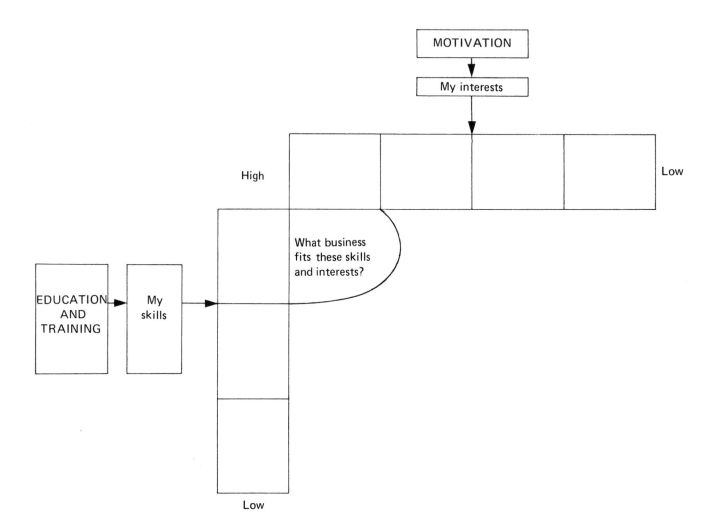

Write *your* high interest and high skills factors in the boxes provided.

Now — What businesses match your high scores?

The seven stages of business start-up

These seven points are designed to help you find where you are, and therefore to see what remains to be done.

At which stage are you?

Tick box when stage is completed

1. Acquiring motivation	Finding the urge and energy to pursue the goal of setting up a business. Checking your own personal capability. *Do you have what it takes?*	☐
2. Finding an idea	Finding an idea on which it seems reasonable to spend *time* and *money* taking further.	☐
3. Proving the idea	Design and manufacture of samples. Testing the product/service technically and with customers. Testing the market. Understanding the market. Protecting the product/service by patents and registered design.	☐
4. Knowing what is needed	Developing the framework for getting into business: ● Premises, cash, equipment, labour. ● The time needed to assemble all the resources. ● Adequate quality control. ● Professional help in starting a business plan (see page 63).	☐
5. Under starter's orders	Applying the business plan. Negotiating for finance, premises, contracts, subcontracts etc. Choosing business name, brand names, the structure (type of company) and registering them. Tax considerations. Use of professional advisers. Getting the right staff. Preparing publicity.	☐
6. The 'off'	First manufacture, first sale. Launch publicity.	☐
7. Staying the course	Keeping track of results. Compare with business plan. Keeping a grip on things. Organising the work. Watching for changes in the market and the law. Keeping the workforce, customers and suppliers happy. Anticipating snags. Improving the product. Looking at competitors.	☐

Note carefully how much more still remains to be done.

Personal preparation

While this checklist is designed to encourage new business start-ups, it also highlights areas where you are apparently ill equipped. Check your answers with your spouse and your business partner.

Yes or No

1. Are your physical health and age compatible with your proposed project?
2. Can you cope mentally with the new stresses and demands?
3. Do you welcome:
    - calculated risks?
    - and responsibility?
4. Have you demonstrated management ability?
5. Do you have the quality of endurance?
6. Can you work alone for sustained periods?
7. Can you accept a reduced income?
8. Will you work without normal financial security?
9. Are you self-confident in the face of adversity and rebuffs?
10. Do you know how many hours per week you wish to work?
11. Do you know how supportive your wife/husband will be?
12. Have you discussed the project with:
    - her/him?
    - the children?
13. Do you appreciate what effect it could have on:
    - family life?
    - the family home?
    - other assets?
14. Have you listed your personal skills?
15. Do you know well the business you are going into?
16. Can you identify what your business project will need from you?
17. Do you know why you want to start the project?
18. Have you set out truthfully what you want out of the business, and when?
19. Will your project affect your personality?
20. Do you know what your attitude is towards
    - paying taxes?
    - long working hours?
    - selling?
    - asking for money?
    - asking for help?
    - power?
    - success?
    - failure?
21. Are there religious, social, educational, or ethical limitations on your business performance?
22. Can you take decisions?
23. Do you get on with people?
24. Have you realistically listed your personal attributes and shortcomings?
25. Will you discuss this listing with an honest and respected friend?

Press on to the next stage of the project if you have truthfully answered 'Yes' to almost every question.

Initial preparation for the business

Now to the business itself. How much do you know about your business area? Use this checklist:

Yes or No

1. Do you have a clear idea of the business opportunity now facing you?

2. Will your product sell?

3. Do you accurately understand your intended product/service?

4. Have you looked at the market for it?

   - What people buy
   - When they buy it
   - Where they buy it
   - Who does the buying
   - Why they should choose your product/service
   - How you will set about selling yours
   - How big the market is for your product
   - Whether it will grow or contract
   - What your share of the market will be

5. Have you checked the moral, legal and environmental objections to your product?

6. Do you know why your product is best?

7. Can you explain this clearly to customers?

8. Will it remain the best?

9. Does it do what you say it does; has it been tested?

10. Will you continue to improve your product?

11. Do you know where new products will come from?

12. Have you sold your product yet?

13. Are you familiar with what customers want?

    - Delivery and after-sales service requirements
    - Quality levels
    - Discount levels

14. Do you know who your competitors are?

15. Do you know what they will do if you enjoy some success?

16. Can you keep up to date with changing techniques and technology?

17. Have you spoken to any potential customers about the market?

18. Do you know what your product will cost to make?

19. Have you calculated your overheads, including selling and distribution?

20. Have you attempted a simple cash flow projection?

21. At this stage do you have an idea of:

    - How much cash you will need in the next 12 months?
    - How much cash you can personally raise?
    - How much external cash you need?
    - When you can repay it?

22. Have you agreed within the family what security you can offer your financiers?

23. Do your partners/shareholders understand your project?

24. Do you know how much it will cost to publicise your product?

25. Do you have:

    - A solicitor?
    - An accountant?
    - A bank manager?
    - Other essential specialists?

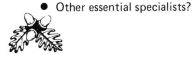

17

26. Have these specialists been properly briefed about the services you require and replied formally about the cost of the service?

27. Have you identified the problems you have never faced before?

The first phase of setting up in business is only completed when you have truthfully **answered 'Yes' to virtually all of these questions.**

Cost of living

Personal and domestic costs have a real bearing on the required financial return from a business venture. This table can be used to help you set personal financial goals to be met by your business.

	Current annual expenses	Economies which can be sustained for a time	Economies which can be made for a lengthy period
Rent or mortgage payments			
Rates			
Food			
Heating, lighting			
House repairs/maintenance			
Personal travel			
Vehicle repairs/maintenance			
Insurances			
Holidays and entertainment			
Clothing			
Subscriptions			
Gifts			
Others —			
—			
—			
TOTAL £			

Now, how much do you need to earn from your business gross, before income tax and National Insurance?

● Per month £
● Per annum £

The final test

In 1984, a second report on business failure under the Loan Guarantee Scheme was prepared by chartered accountants, Robson Rhodes, 'A Study of Business Finance Under the Small Business Loan Guarantee Scheme', published by the Department of Trade and Industry. The authors highlighted shortcomings in the capabilities of proprietors/managers in small business.

Do you avoid these shortcomings?

	How well do you understand:	Does your business plan adequately cover: *Yes or No*
Business finance		
Principal risks to your business		
The competition you will face		
General management of a business		
Marketing		
Production (if applicable)		

How strong is your own record of achievement in industry or commerce?

Unless a realistic assessment of your capabilities gives satisfactory answers to these questions, there are two possible courses of action:

1. Abandon the idea.

2. Take steps to correct weak areas *before* starting the business. For example:

   ● Enrol on a relevant 'Start a Business' course.
   ● Engage qualified professional advisers.
   ● Visit your Local Enterprise Agency or Small Firms Service.
   ● Find partners/shareholders/employees with the required experience.

What Are the Options?

Business start-ups

There is a very limited number of ways of getting into business.

Which best meets the constraints you have in terms of skills, experience, money, property? Has your preferred choice really got a future for you? What about the others?

	In your situation	
	Advantages	*Disadvantages*

1. Buy an existing business

2. Buy the assets of a failed business

3. Put together a new business
   - (a) Very similar to what is already being done
   - (b) Novel or unique product/service

4. Take up a franchise

5. Start a co-operative

Buying a business

The ways in which businesses may be acquired are few in number. This chart sets out the major issues upon which skilled advice should be taken to minimise the risk of loss or unnecessary expense.

Purchaser	Vendor	Method	Watch out for these points
Individual, partnership or company	Sole trader, partnership or company	Acquire assets	Valuation of fixed assets and stock Valuation of goodwill Some assets may not be legally transferable Transfer of patents, trade marks, licences, copyright and other assets Service contracts Vendor responsible for redundancies Freedom of 'old' management to set up in competition
Individual or partnership	Shareholders	Acquire shares	Acquired as a going concern, hence: ● Product liability for old defaults ● Existing contracts maintained including employment ● Pension liabilities taken over ● Obtain warranties and indemnities from vendor ● Liability for debts if trading when insolvent ● Control exercised through shareholders* *A majority shareholding exceeding 50 per cent gives day-to-day control of a company subject to the law of the land and contractual obligations entered into. But some important purposes — notably winding up of the company — require a 75 per cent interest.
Company	Shareholders	Acquire shares — for cash — by issue of shares	As above for individual or partnership, *plus* Consolidation of Group Accounts

In an open market, a business is worth what the highest bidder will pay for it.
It does not follow that this price is fair, right or moral. LOOK OUT!

Buying a shop

Because Britain is alleged to be a 'nation of shopkeepers', and because most shops fail, it is particularly necessary to question your plans.

1. Why do you want to buy a shop? Name your reasons.

Cash
Other reasons

2. What direct competition exists in the area?

3. What indirect competition is there?

   - Mail order
   - Party plan
   - Fairs
   - Markets

4. In the catchment area, what is the:

   - Population
   - Unemployment level
   - Purchasing power

   And their trends?

   What effect might recent or likely changes in these trends have on the business?

5. Is the area to be re-developed?

   (a) Any supermarkets proposed? Will these compete?
   (b) Any road widening or change of traffic flows proposed? Will these compete?
   (c) Will the proximity of suppliers change? With what effect?

6. What are, or will be, the main customer types, eg school children for shops near to schools? Any changes likely?

7. How many people pass the shop each day?

   What proportion of them want your intended product range?

   What will be the size of the average purchase?

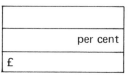

	per cent
£	

8. Walk the streets. Talk to neighbouring shopkeepers, customers and your bank's local manager. Read the local newspapers. Find out all you can about trade in the street and the locality.

9. Note dates of ownership of:

   current owner   19XX – 19XX   Why is he selling?
   prior owner   19XX – 19XX

   What does this information indicate?

22

10. What are current:

sales	£	/week
purchases	£	/week
gross margins by product		per cent

Check till rolls.

Check paying-in books, purchase invoices and delivery notes.
Ignore stories of 'cash into the back pocket'.

11. What do the professionally prepared accounts indicate about:

	This year	Last year	Prior year
Sales	£		
Expenses	£		
Profits	£		

Now do your own forecasts.

12. Check rate of staff turnover. How many will stay on with new owner? Can you recruit new staff successfully?

13. Have comparisons with other shops and businesses been made?

14. What would be the value of the freehold or the lease if property were empty?

15. How much will you need to borrow: £   ?
    Will the business support this borrowing?

16. Have you organised advice from accountants, valuers, solicitors?

17. What hours will you have to work?

    Calculate $\dfrac{\text{Profit}}{\text{Your annual working hours}}$ = £   /hour.

18. Note living accommodation, proximity of schools and churches, recreation facilities, car parks, transport and other social factors.

19. See question 1. Do you still want to buy this shop?
    If so, write down why.

Also do the calculations on page 24.

Current income versus self-employment

It is easy to suppose that self-employment will bring greater income — it rarely does! Try this exercise to see how your project looks.

A	Enter purchase price of business (excluding stock).	£
B	Enter stock as valued.	£
C	Enter cost of improvements needed, if any.	£
D	Enter any other costs, eg legal fees etc.	£
E	Add A, B, C and D together = Total cost of business.	£
F	Enter *net* profit (pre-tax) including any proprietor's salary in last year of business, but be sure you have deducted the bank or loan interest *you* will have to pay.	£
G	Enter *net* profit (pre-tax) estimated for *next* year including proprietor's salary, but be sure you have deducted the bank or loan interest *you* will have to pay.	£
H	Enter current interest paid on present cash on deposit or other investments to be sold.	£ £
I	Enter your present annual earnings or social security payments.	£
J	Add H and I together.	£
K	Deduct J from F = Benefit from running business (calculated on current earnings).	£
L	K ÷ E x 100 = Return on investment (calculated on current earnings).	%
M	Deduct J from G = Benefit from running business (calculated on estimated earnings).	£
N	M ÷ E x 100 = Return on investment (calculated on estimated future earnings).	%

There are other valid reasons for starting a business. What are yours?

But **don't forget these figures.**

Taking up a franchise

With successful franchises like Prontaprint and Dyno-Rod as examples, observers expect that franchises will increase in importance as opportunities for new business start-ups. Because they have a much higher survival rate, franchises are viewed favourably by outside investors, notably the banks. To aid the would-be franchisee, these checklists have been prepared.

Tick when checked

1. *Business environment*

   (a) Analyse own motivation and capabilities. ☐

   (b) Review commitment of the immediate family to the idea. ☐

   (c) Assess public awareness and acceptability of franchised product. ☐

   (d) Check protection of product by patents, trade marks, copyrights. ☐

   (e) Look for strong possibility of expanded use of product. ☐

   (f) Review strength of competition, franchised or otherwise. ☐

   (g) Examine pricing. ☐

2. *Franchisor*

   (a) Find out length of time and experience in franchising in the UK. ☐

   (b) Obtain the bank status report and latest audited accounts. ☐

   (c) Look at the management structure. ☐

   (d) Review communication systems and effectiveness. ☐

   (e) Contact other existing franchisees. ☐

   (f) Get comments on operations manual. ☐

   (g) Note payments to franchisor: fee, royalty, levy. ☐

3. *Franchise agreement*

   (a) Note terms and conditions of renewal. ☐

   (b) Look at franchisor's and franchisee's obligations. ☐

   (c) Check out franchisor's accountability regarding advertising and other levies. ☐

   (d) Examine franchise sale options. ☐

   (e) Note minimum sales quantity requirement and other termination clauses. ☐

   (f) Understand exclusivity of territories. ☐

   (g) Note compulsory death and incapacity covers. ☐

   (h) VAT liabilities on fees, royalties etc. ☐

Setting up a franchise

The franchisor will eventually sell a package of *proven* know-how relating to a specific type of business activity. With the package the franchisor is likely to attract sound franchisees and the necessary finance: 12 months may well be necessary to complete this development programme.

1. Eliminate as soon as possible the risks inherent in any business start-up by thoroughly market testing a small number of pilot operations.

2. Provide the means by which the franchisee can be his own boss.

3. Develop a detailed operational manual setting out how the business should be run.

4. Develop strong branding of the franchise through media appropriate to the franchise's target market.

5. Prepare the franchise prospectus to show anticipated returns on investment.

6. Obtain Newspaper Publishers Association approval prior to advertising for franchisees (Newspaper Publishers Association Ltd, 6 Bouverie Street, London EC4Y 8AY; telephone 01-583 8132), but this is probably dealt with through the publication you choose.

7. Protect intellectual property: patents, trade marks, copyrights.

8. Prepare the franchise agreement with a solicitor experienced in this field.

9. Obtain in-principle support from the franchise specialist units in the major banks.

10. Consider joining the British Franchise Association: Franchise Chambers, 75a Bell Street, Henley-on-Thames, Oxon RG9 2BD; telephone 0491 578049.

Worker co-operatives

What is a worker co-operative?

A worker co-operative is basically a business owned and controlled by those who work in it.

Each member has an equal say, either in the running of the co-operative, or in the election of a management committee.

Profits are shared by the members in proportion to the work put in by each.

Who starts a worker co-operative?

People with an idea for a marketable product or service, and the skills, experience and enthusiasm needed to work together.

People who want to work for themselves as equals and share the rewards in an equitable way and at the same time create useful employment.

People who want to work locally and keep profits in the community.

People who are unemployed, in danger of becoming so, or in need of part-time work.

Companies that see their employees as partners and wish to improve motivation and job satisfaction can convert to worker co-operatives.

How do you go about it?

The Co-operative Development Agency (CDA) can extend its help to those wanting to set up a worker co-operative. Contact the CDA direct at Broadmead House, 21 Panton Street, London SW1Y 4DR; telephone 01-839 2988, or through the local enterprise agency.

CDA will advise you on what is necessary to get going, discuss the demand for your product or service, help you to draw up a business plan and prepare loan applications, help find suitable premises and guide you through legal and tax matters.

CDA also have available ready-made rules for co-operatives, which have been tried and tested throughout the UK to ease the process of registration.

Chapter 3

What Has to be Done? Who Will Help?

Countdown to start-up

This list outlines matters to be resolved before a business can start trading. Use the boxes to indicate what you have completed.

	Date done	See also page

1. Note the addresses and phone numbers of local business advisers such as:
   - Small Firms Service
   - Council for Small Industries in Rural Areas
   - Local Enterprise Agency
   - Small Business Club

   Check availability of local courses on starting a business.   35, 36, 38

2. Research and understand the market for your product.   95, 96

3. Establish preliminary product costings.

4. Review the seven qualifications for the Enterprise Allowance Scheme (Jobcentre leaflet). If appropriate, book in for an 'information session' through the Jobcentre. *Don't* start trading until accepted on to the scheme, if you are eligible.   29-30

5. Appoint your accountant; agree service and fee. Establish business records systems.   29-30

6. Appoint your solicitor; agree service and fee. Review the form of your business.   82

7. Select business name.   72, 73, 76

8. Find and cost premises. Consult Fire Brigade about expenses associated with obtaining a Fire Certificate.   72, 77-9

9. Check with Planning Office, District or Borough Council, about planning and building regulations constraints on the property/home. Note restrictions on the use of advertising signs.   29, 30

10. Advise your bank manager of your plans.   86

11. Determine what licences, certificates and the like will be necessary to permit you to trade.   87-9

12. Investigate patent, registered design, trade mark and copyright protection. Apply for protection if justifiable.   70

13. Check the availability of grant aid for your business.   92

14. Locate key suppliers, confirm their prices and deliveries.   38-9

15. Establish your prices and discounts.   63-5

16. Complete the business plan, including 12-month financial plan. NB. Ensure business plan includes sufficient cash being available to cover the requirement of the first 12 months.   60

17. Obtain from bank written confirmation of loan/overdraft facilities. Seek to understand how arrangement fees, bank charges and interest will be charged. Open the bank account.   80-83

18. If applicable, form a company or draw up a partnership agreement.   30-31, 74-5

19. For business premises, take professional advice on leases, purchase and licences.

	Date done	See also page

20. Apply for and obtain permission to trade where necessary (see also 11 above). — 77-9

21. Inform Inspector of Taxes that you are starting in business, preferably through your accountant, using Form 41G. Provide him with your P45. Read booklet IR28 'Setting up in Business'. — 39, 85

22. Inform Department of Health and Social Security (DHSS) for National Insurance purposes. Check Family Income Supplement option. — 103-5

23. Establish income tax and National Insurance contribution deductions using appropriate forms. Be familiar with Statutory Sick Pay (SSP) Scheme. — 103-6

24. Contact VAT Office and, if necessary, establish records and registration (in telephone directory under Customs and Excise). — 84

25. Confirm mail and telephone links with Post Office and British Telecom. — 101-2

26. Plan communications of product/service to your target market. — 40-47

27. Make sure appropriate insurance covers are taken out. — 85

28. Establish terms and conditions of employment. Note the requirement to maintain existing terms and conditions where an existing business is being taken over. — 103-5

29. Contact Jobcentre regarding future employees. Consider Youth Training Scheme. — 106

30. Take delivery of all business stationery and promotional materials. — 40, 90

31. Advise the Rating Department of your District or Borough Council. Check options to pay monthly and half yearly. Avoid paying rates on empty premises.

32. Factories: advise Health and Safety Executive.

33. Shops and offices: complete and return Form OSR1 to Environmental Health and Housing Department, District or Borough Council. — 86

34. Ensure mains services are connected to your premises: — 73,76

   - Gas
   - Electricity (single/three phase)
   - Water
   - Drainage

35. For credit or hire sales, apply to Trading Standards Office.

36. Prepare launch of the business with press/media support.

37. Take out bank and credit references for major new, unknown credit customers. Think twice about some known credit customers. — 40-47

38. Consider joining the: — 98

   - Small Business Club
   - Chamber of Commerce, or equivalent
   - Chamber of Trade
   - Trade Association, eg Master Builders, Licensed Victuallers

Selection of professional advisers

All small businesses should seek cost-effective contributions to the management of their business from appropriate professional advisers.

Key professions include accountants, solicitors, estate agents and bank managers.

The best times to make the choice are:

- before the business begins operations
- before a new phase in the development of the business.

The steps in the selection process are:

1. Make appointments and visit at least two, preferably three, of each class of adviser.
2. Discuss your business opportunity. Agree with the adviser the list of services he can provide to meet business needs.
3. Agree the dates by which the services will be provided.
4. Discuss the cost of the service and the terms of payment for it.
5. Obtain confirmation in writing of points 2, 3 and 4.
6. Make your selection on the basis of the written confirmation and the personal interview.
7. Courteously advise the prospective advisers of your choice.

Services available from your advisers

The checklists will help you to see what your advisers can do for you. It is your job to ensure that you get value for money spent on buying their services.

Accountant

Your accountant should be a vital member of your small management team.

- Company formation
- Partnership agreements
- Accounting/Bookkeeping systems
- Value Added Tax (VAT)
- Pay as you Earn (PAYE)/National Insurance administration
- Government grants
- Business planning including budgets and forecasts
- Cash raising
- Management information
- Interim accounts preparation
- Year-end accounts preparation
- Annual audit
- Capital restructuring
- Business tax
- Business tax planning
- Company secretarial services
- Personal tax
- Personal tax planning
- Pension arrangements/schemes
- Disability arrangements
- Death cover
- Retirement planning
- Investment planning

29

- Capital Transfer Tax planning
- Wills
- Receiverships and liquidations

Solicitor

Your solicitor will prove to be of vital importance on occasions during the formation, growth and, perhaps, the winding up of your business. Agree the service(s) to be provided.

- Tailormade company formation and registration
- Partnership agreements. A written agreement covering basic terms is advisable.
- Property — freehold and lease negotiations and conveyancing
- Employment law, eg contracts of employment
- Commercial law, eg agency appointments
- Debt collection
- Inter-company disputes
- Distribution, licensing, secrecy, manufacturing agreements
- Patents and copyright
- Terms of trade
- Personal guarantees.

Bank

Your bank is a very necessary part of your business from the start. A vast organisation of specialists is available to guide you in the financial planning of your business, and on the best use of funds.

A short guide to possible facilities available:

- *Current account.* For day-to-day trading.
- *Deposit account.* For investment of surplus funds — special rates for larger deposits.
- *Loan account* (long term). Capital borrowings repaid over period of years.
- *Assistance in importing and exporting.* Advice on methods, finance; economic intelligence reports on countries worldwide.
- *Provision of finance.* Overdraft, loans, discounting, bills of exchange, medium-term loans, business start-up loans, business expansion loans, government Loan Guarantee Scheme.
- *Leasing/factoring services.* Through specialist bank subsidiaries.
- *Transmission of funds.* Credit transfers, overseas payments, direct debit system etc.

Your local manager is available to give on-the-spot advice in all matters relating to the financial aspect of your business.

Architect

Your architect is a valuable member of the building team in the construction of new premises and the alteration of existing buildings.

His work includes site investigation, feasibility studies, obtaining planning consents, investigation into problems of strength, construction, weather proofing, energy conservation etc.

An architect knows the best way through all the problems and regulations associated with building, and will look after your interests through all or any stages of a building project.

Services supplied by your architect may include:

- *New buildings.* Investigation of site, town planning problems, feasibility studies including estimates of the cost of the project, sketch plans, working drawings, obtaining competitive quotations, preparing contracts, supervising the work to completion.
- *Old buildings.* In addition to the services listed above for new buildings, your architect may be able to complete feasibility studies regarding alterations and improvements.
- *Grant work.* Advising on any grants available.

- *Litigation.* Providing technical expertise in building dispute cases.

- *Energy saving.* Advising on economies in heating of properties and on any grants and other such help available to meet the costs of new installations to achieve energy saving.

- *Advice on leases on purchase of property.* Advice can be given on the conditions attached to purchases on leases, including the preparation of schedules of conditions to be incorporated in any lease.

Services available from a surveyor and most estate agents

Where bank lending is to finance the purchase of a property, the bank will require a valuation of that property by a reputable valuation surveyor. Sometimes banks recommend a valuer; others let you choose your own. If you choose your own, advise the bank of your choice at an early stage. Always choose a member of the Royal Institution of Chartered Surveyors (RICS) or the Incorporated Society of Valuers and Auctioneers (ISVA).

The surveyor will also be able to advise on the following:

If you are buying:

- Structural condition of the property

- Whether or not the rating assessment is too high

- Defective workmanship

- Whether or not planning permission is required and making the application.

If you are leasing:

- The condition of the property and make recommendations. Modern leases usually make the tenant responsible for all repairs; with older buildings the implications can be immense. A surveyor will advise on schedules of condition and negotiate your lease terms.

- Rating

- Planning permission

- Negotiating the rent at the commencement of the lease or upon rent review.

The surveyor will also be able to recommend other associated professions who can give more detailed advice on heating, electrical installations, and building design.

Insurance adviser

Your insurance adviser is important at all stages of your business career, from initial planning onwards. He will help you to ensure the continuation of your business and your income should accidents occur, and also ensure that you meet any legal requirements, eg public liability insurance.

Certain areas of insurance such as life and pensions require a specialist adviser.

When you seek his advice you should cover the areas listed below. Choose an adviser who is helpful, efficient, and in whom you can trust.

- *General*
  Accident, fire, theft, vehicles, stock, equipment etc

- *Business*
  Liability and consequential loss

- *Sickness*
  Personal accident, temporary/permanent disability, private medical care

- *Death*
  Of key personnel, shareholder, owner or partner

- *Pension*
  Directors, employers, employees
  State, insured and self-administered schemes

- *Loans*
  Alongside pension or pension loanback

- *Personal investment planning*
  Your capital and/or income requirements or
  aims outside direct business growth.

If the insurance covers are to be arranged through a broker, be sure to enquire about the insurance company with which the business is placed. The most reliable service may be provided by members of the British Insurance Association, Aldermary House, Queen Street, London EC4 4JD; telephone 01-248 4477.

31

Design consultant
Design has a vital, often misunderstood, role in improving profitability.

	Yes or No
1. Will design improve my share of the intended, or existing market?	_____
2. Will design reduce manufacturing costs?	_____
3. Will design improve the product?	_____
4. Will design improve cash flow, net of costs?	_____

Where good design will answer 'Yes' to these questions, contact a designer, looking for these particular points:

(a) Designer should spend enough time learning about you and your business.

(b) Obtain a 'no obligation' proposal of design work founded on the areas already agreed in discussions.

(c) Ensure your designer submits the proposal accurately describing work undertaken, in stages, with time and costs clearly shown.

(d) Brilliance is no substitute for experience, so choose a designer with a track record. Ask for references; discover whether the design experience is suitable to your need.

Then:

(e) Payment should be made only after a satisfactory completion of each stage.

In some cases, design assistance may be available under the Design Council's Design Advisory Service Funded Consultancy Scheme. Details are available from the Design Council, 28 Haymarket, London SW1Y 4SU; telephone 01-839 8000.

Public relations consultant
The PR task is to help you devise your company message, to select who receives it, and to make sure that you communicate that company message to the target group in the outside world.

● *Press relations*
The most common form of PR. Prepare your message, usually in the form of a press release about your product, despatch to the relevant media (newspapers, magazines, trade journals, radio or TV); could involve a press reception or arrange special events to attract media attention.

● *Corporate PR*
Will help you describe your company to the outside world: could take the form of a company brochure, film or video; may involve research into how other people (eg your suppliers or customers) see you and how to change their views (or yours) for the better.

● *Lobbying*
Is intended to change the view of a legislative body, eg Parliament, EEC committees, the Town Hall, your union executive, by preparing a case for their consideration. Methods include: arranging special meetings, personal contact, public exposure.

● *Financial PR*
Is intended to attract investors to your company. Work with brokers and merchant banks to ensure the correct company profile or to attract attention in the specialist financial media.

● *Industrial PR*
Helps you explain company activities to your employees. It can take the form of a company newsletter, open days, sponsorship of sports teams or local events.

PR FOR NEW COMPANIES
A new company needs to identify its 'publics'. Who would influence the success of your business? Is it the Town Hall, the local residents, employees, an untapped market, a trade union or a government department?

PR consultancies can help you with a wide variety of marketing and management tasks. Larger companies employ specialists in market research, audio-visual production, management consultancy, promotions and advertising, but a smaller company can get this advice from their PR consultancy. Writing customer letters, sales leaflets or video scripts, for example, is often the area where a PR consultancy is particularly helpful.

Advertising agent
It is probably *more important for a small firm to make effective use of its promotional funds than it is for a large company.*
A well chosen and well briefed advertising agency can make a big contribution to this work.

A 'full service' advertising agency will handle:

- *Research.* Market, advertising, pricing, pack

- *Campaign presentation.* Artwork, layout, copy, media, design

- *Implementation.* Production, media buying, delivery, insertions, monitoring of costs and effectiveness

- *Sales promotion.* Pack, deals

- *Merchandising/Display.* Point of sale work

- *Development.* Product, market

- *Forecasting.* Sales, mathematical modelling

- *Exhibitions.* Stand design and management

- *Public relations.* Media, lobbying.

Smaller agencies may handle just one or two of the functions listed.

The small business client should approach his briefing of the advertising on the basis of:

- Knowing the *product benefits*

- Knowing the *target market* — the customer

- Knowing what the advertising must do.

Dealing with your local council

Executives or officials employed by the council have delegated powers enabling them to take decisions which may affect your business. In other cases the powers are retained by sub-committees or the council itself, which may accept or reject advice provided by the officers. To benefit your business you should know who takes the decision and how.

These charts show typical executive and committee structures in a local council.

Committee structure of a typical District or Borough Council

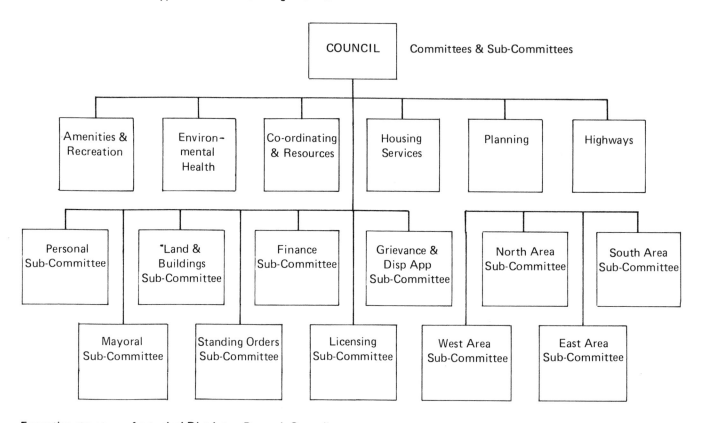

Executive structure of a typical District or Borough Council

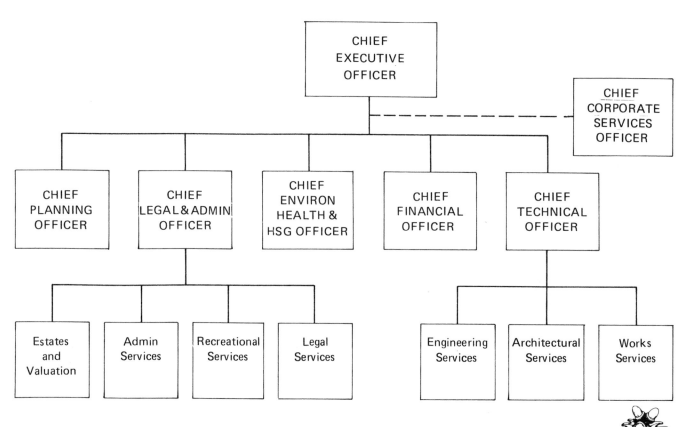

Chapter 4

No Customers-
No Business

Market research for the small business

Whatever your talents are, skilled craftsman, top executive, butcher, baker or candlestick maker, all have one thing in common — *no customers, no business.* A vague idea that there are lots of people out there who need me is a pleasant thought and good for the ego — but it won't pay the rent, and it won't convince your bank manager to lend you money.

The way to understand better whether customers truly exist is to ask the right questions:

1. How many *potential* customers are there?
2. How many *real* customers are there?
3. Who are they?
4. Who does the buying?
5. Where is the buying done?
6. Where are the customers?
7. What kind of product or service do they want to buy?
8. Why do they want the product or service?
9. Where do they get it at present?
10. How much will they want to pay?
11. What deficiencies do the current products or services have?
12. When do customers buy, how much and how frequently?
13. Can you deliver what they want when they want it?
14. Who else can supply this product/service?
15. How strong is this competition?
16. Will the market grow or contract?

The answers to questions may be found by:

(a) *'Desk' research.* Newspapers, advertisements, libraries, reference works, textbooks, market surveys.
(b) *Visiting potential retailers/distributors.* Talking to them in a pre-planned way, finding out prices and discounts.
(c) *Visiting competitors.* Talking to them, obtaining literature, price-lists and samples.
(d) *Observing similar establishments.* Customer flow.
(e) *Visiting users.* Discussing what benefits they associate with your product or product type.

Such contacts may be made by:

● Personal visit — the best.
● Telephone — but only by a skilled person aided by a written guideline.
● Mail questionnaire — but expect a low response.

Part of the market research is quite properly descriptive — 'feel' — and is described as *qualitative* research. For analysts such as bank managers and business advisers, there is also a vital requirement for numbers: *quantitative* research.

For would-be retailers, traffic flow into the shop is vital. Research location!

Sources of market information

In the preparation for the business start-up, it can be easy to neglect the opportunity to check published information — often available free of charge — which may allow the market size, trends, prices and customers to be identified.

Agricultural Statistics, HMSO

Annual Abstract of Statistics, HMSO

Bank of England Quarterly Bulletin, Bank of England

British Business, HMSO

British Monitors, HMSO

County, Borough and Town Profiles, County and District Councils (various)

County Council Industrial Registers, County Councils (various)

Digest of UK Energy Statistics, HMSO

Dun & Bradstreet Directories, Dun & Bradstreet

Economic Trends, HMSO

Employment Gazette, HMSO

European Marketing Data and Statistics, Euromonitor

Family Expenditure Survey, HMSO

Financial Statistics, HMSO

General Household Survey, HMSO

Inland Revenue Statistics, HMSO

Jordan's Industry Sector, Jordans Ltd

Kelly's Directories, Kelly's

Key Note Business Reports, Key Note Publications

Kompass Directories, Kompass UK

Local Government Trends, HMSO

Mintel Market Intelligence, Mintel

Monthly Digest of Statistics, HMSO

National Income and Expenditure, HMSO

National Institute Economic Review, National Institute for Economic & Social Research

OECD Main Economic Indicators, HMSO

Regional Trends, HMSO

Retail Business, HMSO

Social Trends, HMSO

Transport Statistics, HMSO

UN Statistical Yearbook, HMSO/United Nations Organisation

Yellow Pages, British Telecom

Have you visited your local library? Much of this information is waiting for you there.

Product pricing

Avoiding the temptation to establish prices on the basis of internal costs, the successful business:

1. Researches prices and discounts in the market

2. Remembers that price is an attribute of the market *and* product or service

3. Assesses other elements in the competition — notably quality and delivery

4. Knows that it is easier to reduce a price than to put it up.

For a conventional manufactured product sold by wholesale and retail distribution, this price schedule may help you to price your product in the market-place.

	Main competitors									Your product	
	1			2			3			Initial price	Adjusted price
Name of product · Main retailer											
	Pack size			Pack size			Pack size				
	A	B	C	A	B	C	A	B	C		
Recommended retail price											
Marketed price											
Actual selling price											
Trade price* Volume discounts											
Net trade price*											
Wholesale price* Volume discounts											
Net wholesale price*											
Quality rating											
Delivery rating											
Other ratings											

* It may be difficult to get all this information.

Price as an attribute of the product or service

It is too easy, and bad business, to think that the new product or service has to be the cheapest.

This table encourages you to compare your products with your competitors. Tick as appropriate.

Comparison with competitors

Tick which product attributes are most important to the customer

Product attributes	Worse −3 −2 −1	Same 0	Better +1 +2 +3	
Design				
Performance				
Packaging				
Presentation/ appearance				
After-sales service				
Availability				
Delivery				
Colour/flavour/ odour/touch				
Image				
Specification				
Payment terms				
Others:				

Now look again at:

Discounts

Price

And now, at your costs

Discounts and price changes

Discounts
Suppliers may offer cash discounts for prompt payment of outstanding bills. Use this table to see how the cost of the deal compares with overdraft or loan interest rates.

		Annual interest rate % to break even (pre-tax) (Cost in %)						
		Extra credit taken — in weeks						
Discount forgone: %	5	6	7	8	9	10	11	12
1	10.5	8.7	7.5	6.6	5.8	5.2	4.8	4.4
1½	15.8	13.1	11.3	9.9	8.8	7.9	7.2	6.6
2	21.1	17.6	15.1	13.2	11.7	10.5	9.6	8.8
2½	26.4	22.0	18.9	16.5	14.7	13.2	12.0	11.0
3	31.8	26.5	22.7	19.9	17.7	15.9	14.4	13.2
5	53.5	44.6	38.2	33.5	29.7	26.8	24.3	22.3

Price reductions
Cut the price to increase sales volume. Before you do, check that sales volume increase needed to break even (ignoring the costs of handling increased sales volumes) really will happen. Beware of setting off a price war with your competitors; it is the route to ruin for you all.

	Percentage sales volume increase needed to break even on a price reduction					
	Gross margins (%)					
Price reduction	15	20	25	30	35	40
1%	7.1	5.3	4.2	3.5	2.9	2.6
5%	50.0	33.3	25.0	20.0	16.7	14.3
10%	200.0	100.0	67.7	50.0	40.0	33.3
15%	—	300.0	150.0	100.0	75.0	60.0

Price increases
As a corollary, look at the sales volume reductions which a price increase will support. It is more profitable to sell fewer items at a higher price.

	Percentage sales volume decrease supported by a price increase					
	Gross Margins (%)					
Price reduction	15	20	25	30	35	40
1%	6.3	4.8	3.9	3.2	2.8	2.4
5%	25.0	20.0	16.7	14.3	12.5	11.1
10%	40.0	33.3	28.6	25.0	22.2	20.0
15%	50.0	42.9	37.5	33.3	30.0	27.3

Marketing

Marketing of products or services is relatively more important for small businesses than it is in the case of the giant fast-moving consumer goods companies like Procter & Gamble.

Marketing means the consistent, coherent communication of benefits derived from the product or service to the consumer.

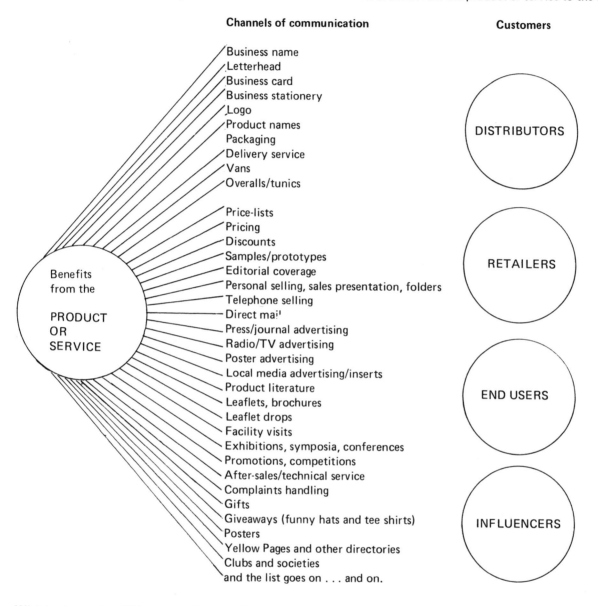

Channels of communication

Business name
Letterhead
Business card
Business stationery
Logo
Product names
Packaging
Delivery service
Vans
Overalls/tunics

Price-lists
Pricing
Discounts
Samples/prototypes
Editorial coverage
Personal selling, sales presentation, folders
Telephone selling
Direct mail
Press/journal advertising
Radio/TV advertising
Poster advertising
Local media advertising/inserts
Product literature
Leaflets, brochures
Leaflet drops
Facility visits
Exhibitions, symposia, conferences
Promotions, competitions
After-sales/technical service
Complaints handling
Gifts
Giveaways (funny hats and tee shirts)
Posters
Yellow Pages and other directories
Clubs and societies
and the list goes on . . . and on.

Benefits from the **PRODUCT OR SERVICE**

Customers

DISTRIBUTORS

RETAILERS

END USERS

INFLUENCERS

Which channels will be cost effective for your business?

Promote benefits to the customer

You know what you make. Do you know what your customers buy?
Use this schedule to link the features you expensively build into your product or service to real benefits to your customers.

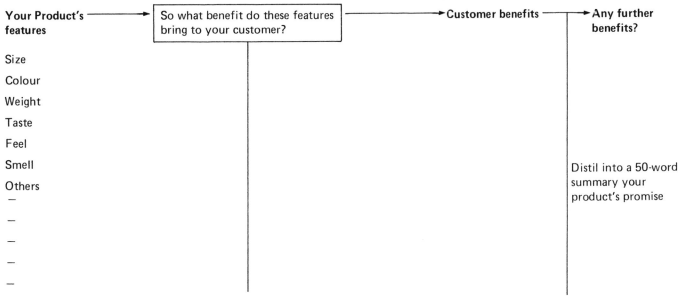

Your Product's features	So what benefit do these features bring to your customer?	Customer benefits	Any further benefits?
Size			
Colour			
Weight			
Taste			
Feel			
Smell			Distil into a 50-word summary your product's promise
Others			
—			
—			
—			
—			
—			

Selling, advertising and promotion should be based on the important customer benefits

Your target market

The target market is the group — or groups — of individuals to whom your business most succesfully communicates its key messages in order for you to succeed.

Define your target market by:

- Age
- Sex
- Location
- Social group
- Job title or occupation
- Special interests
- Life style
- Events/features
- Seasonality
- Other important descriptions

Estimated number of individuals making up target group in your location:

Are there other target markets useful to your business which you can define?

Choosing your advertising medium

Selection of the best advertising medium is for the most part based on the costs of hitting the agreed target market. This table will allow media cost comparisons to be made.

NB. Origination, artwork and production costs must also be assessed.

Where figures are difficult to obtain, some low-cost experimentation will be necessary. Monitoring of results is, of course, even more important than usual.

PRINT	Audited circulation	Researched readership	Target market readership	Cost per 1000 target market	How does this medium relate to your product/service?
Newspapers					
Journals					

BROADCASTING	Audience research	Target market audience	Cost per 1000 target market	How does this medium relate to your product/service?
Radio				
Television				
Cable television				
Cinema				

DIRECT SELLING	List and delivery research	Target market delivery	Cost per 1000 target market	How does this medium relate to your product/service?
Direct mail				
Leafleting				
Telephone selling				

SHOWS AND EXHIBITIONS	Attendance	Target market attendance	Cost per 1000 target market	How does this medium relate to your product/service?
Shows				
Exhibitions				
Conferences				

Monitoring of local advertising

Direct response advertising (including coupons) lends itself to ready cost-effectiveness comparisons. This information should be collected for every campaign as a means of improving future campaigns.

This same table may be easily adapted to monitor direct mail and telephone sales campaigns.

Publication												
Frequency*												
Circulation (000s) (a)												
Number of insertions (b)												
Cost per insertion £ (c)												
Cost per 000 circulation £	$\frac{c}{a}$											
Cost of campaign £ (d)=	bxc											
Number of enquiries (e)												
Number of quotations (f)												
Number of orders (g)												
Value of orders (h)												
Cost per enquiry £	$\frac{d}{e}$											
Cost per order £	$\frac{d}{g}$											
Cost per £ order value	$\frac{d}{h}$											

*Quarterly, monthly, weekly or daily

PRESS RELEASE

Macclesfield Business Ventures

Registered Office. Venture House, Cross Street, Macclesfield SK11 7PG. Telephone 0625 615113

FREE ADVERTISING THROUGH EDITORIAL

Small businesses are full of news. News about people, products, premises, policies and progress. But surprisingly, the low cost promotional opportunities through news releases are neglected by small business.

To put this right, build a story round people and their success. Keep to the facts. Write the story in short sentences. Summarise the story in the first paragraph. Get the story typed with wide margins, double spaced. Include interesting quotations from key people. Avoid underlining and indiscriminate use of capital letters. Spell numbers one to nine, thereafter use figures. Use eight inch by five inch black and white photographs where possible. But photographs need clear accurate captions attached to them.

Select your target publications to include local, regional and national press, appropriate trade and technical publications, radio and television. Be sure to get your material to them by their copy date.

ENDS . . .

Contact: Name   Phone
             Address

                                      Date

Direct mail reduces marketing costs and gains new customers

Macclesfield Business Ventures

Registered Office. Venture House, Cross Street, Macclesfield SK11 7PG. Telephone 0625 615113

Mr J Smith
Managing Director
Buggins Ltd
Industrial Estate
Newtown NW1T 0WN

Dear Mr Smith

Would you like to reduce marketing costs? Would you like new customers?

For small but growing businesses like yours, DIRECT MAIL can be the most cost-effective way of bringing in new business.

Using bought-in mailing lists costing between £50 and £100 per thousand addresses, your message can be accurately delivered to your best prospects for between £200 and £300 per thousand. Using your own existing customer lists may be both cheaper and provide a better response.

These are the main questions for you to consider:

* What is the message to be communicated?
* What action do you want your prospect to take?
* What steps will you take to make it easy for your prospect to reply?
* What plans do you have to follow up non-responders?
* Have you the capacity and staff to handle the replies?
* What response rate are you expecting?
* Is the expense likely to produce a profit benefit?

> Experience in direct marketing by mail shows that mailings which arrive with your prospect on Tuesdays obtain the best response rates. Most successful direct marketers avoid holiday periods and 'silly seasons'.

CAPITALS, underlining, asterisks and postscripts all improve the chances of bringing in the business. Of course, keep it simple. Use short sentences. A personalized greeting, as in this letter, Mr Smith, and a legible signature, also help response rates.

Telephone your marketing adviser NOW to set up a small test campaign.

Yours sincerely

A. Seller

A. Seller

PS   Did you know that the Post Office have free introductory offers on first mail shots and Business Reply licences? Get the facts from their Sales Office TODAY.

Methods of selling

Even the one-person company must sell hard. From the almost limitless list of sales opportunities, 24 of the most common are reviewed below.

	To the trade	To the public	Comments	Estimate the cost
Personal visit	✓	✓	Gets in the way of other activities.	
Salesman	✓	?	Can be difficult to control.	
Sales agent	✓	✓	Paid according to results.	
Telephone sales	✓	✓	New skill?	
Mailing	✓	✓	Low response rate. Can be targeted.	
Poster		✓	Cheap to produce. Costly to post.	
Radio	?	✓	Good for special segments of the market.	
Television	?	✓	Expensive for small business. NB. Channel 4.	
Newspapers	?	✓	Good cover. Wasted readership.	
Journals Trade and technical General interest Special interest	✓ ?	? ✓✓	Response may be measurable	
Leaflets/brochures				
Mail order		✓	Difficult to get into catalogue.	
Shows/exhibitions Trade General	✓	✓	Sometimes essential. Beware of unprofitable turnover.	
Directories	✓	?	Yellow Pages and similar.	
Party plan		✓	Beware of pyramid selling.	
Cinema	?	✓	Declining audiences. Good for some segments.	
In-store demonstrations		✓	Good visibility — check sales/profits.	
Shop window cards	?	✓	Useful for trades/skills of local interest.	
Sampling/trial use	✓	?	Expensive. May help an excellent product.	
Editorial	✓	✓	Often overlooked — almost free.	
Facility visits	✓	?	Visits to premises.	
Complaints	✓	✓	Always a new sales opportunity.	
Conferences	✓		Useful for specialised technical message.	
Competitions/promotions	✓	✓	Can bring life to a dull product.	

Exhibitions and shows

Effective participation in a well chosen exhibition can work wonders for a small, little known business seeking new business with individual, small, medium-sized and larger businesses. Common problems include:

- Choosing an unsuitable exhibition
- Underestimating the manpower and costs involved in the exhibition
- Forgetting to brief staff on the purpose of being there
- Omitting to follow up on all interested contacts after the exhibition.

Put simply,
exhibitions
are:

Horizontal	or	Appealing to a wide cross section of the population: Business to Business Exhibition Royal Show Ideal Homes Exhibition
	Vertical	
	Appealing in depth to a specific audience: Cruft's Dog Show Congress of Cardiology Offshore Inspection Repair and Maintenance Exhibition	

What local
    regional
    national
exhibitions meet your business needs?

What are the costs involved?	
Space hire	£
Stand design	£
building	£
services	£
fitting	£
Manning costs: people x cost/day	£
Additional print material and gifts	£
Travel, entertainment, accommodation	£
Total	£
+ Costs of not doing other priority things	£

What are your objectives?	
Direct sales off the stand	£
Lead generation	Number:
Product enquiries	Number:
Product launch	
How will follow-up be done?	

Now you can measure the cost-effectiveness of your stand.

How many customers?

Answer: Fewer than you might first imagine

Estimated annual sales	£	(a)
Average size of sales transaction	£	(b)
∴ Annual number of sales transactions (a) ÷ (b)		(c)
Average annual frequency of customer purchase		(d)
∴ Annual number of customers* (c) ÷ (d)		(e)
Number of existing customers		(f)
Number of new customers needed (e) — (f)	_____	

* For very small business, this number often lies in the range:

30 — for special trade selling operations

to

300 — for retail shops

BUT harder to obtain than you would ever have thought.

Now look at the sales cascade (next page).

The sales cascade

In business start-ups and expansions, it is easy to overlook the workload in generating new business.

Estimate your conversion rates, then calculate leads, contacts and interviews in order to meet your sales targets.

The number of interviews vary with the type of product or its market.	Conversion rates from one level to the next		Number required to meet your sales plan		Time/cost involved £ or hours
	Typical	*Your business*			
Success One order	3	☐	☐	Orders/ customers required	
Third interview Final bid for the business			☐	Third interviews	
Second interview Handling objections Confirming details	1.5	☐	☐	Second interviews	
First interview The initial sales presentation	1.5	☐	☐	First interviews	
Contacts Conversation with named, relevant person, often prelude to an appointment	3	☐	☐	Contacts	
Leads An address, phone number, possibly a name. Can you generate sufficient?	5	☐	☐	Leads	
Multiplier effect	101.25				

Selling to large buyers

Most large organisations, such as ICI, Shell, and local authorities, are keen to encourage the development of new small suppliers. But almost all of them need to be satisfied about the reliability and financial stability of the supplier.

The following form is reproduced from the Cheshire County Council procedure for becoming an approved supplier.

To: CONTROLLER OF SUPPLIES CHESHIRE COUNTY COUNCIL	APPLICATION FOR INCLUSION ON THE COUNTY'S SELECT LIST OF CONTRACTORS
1. Name of applicant (individual or organisation)	To be completed by the applicant
2. Address for normal business	
3. State whether independent, or whether subsidiary or member of group	
4. Turnover in £ sterling in respect of main goods (or services) being offered	
5. Percentage that above represents in relation to the overall turnover	
6. Specialities offered (goods or services)	
7. Extent of technical or other services available to your customers (as applicable). (a) technical, (b) maintenance (c) design	(a) (b) (c)
8. Name other local authorities from whom you have been awarded contracts during past five years (state full addresses)	
9. Other public organisations to whom you are currently supplying goods or services (state full addresses)	(a) (b) (c) .
10. Value of such contracts	8(a) 8(b) 8(c) 9(a) 9(b) 9(c)
11. Any other relevant information which will aid the Controller of Supplies in the consideration of your application	

Sales control

To encourage attention to selling, this daily activity report has been drawn up. Even the one-person business can use the report, doing so for those days or part days in the week when active selling is done.

Daily activity report					Date								
Customer*	**Call type** C or I		**New(N) or existing (E) customer**	**Order size £**	**Products detailed*** 1	2	3	4	5	6	7		**Information******
*****	TOTAL C = TOTAL N = TOTAL I = TOTAL E = TOTAL V = TOTAL T =			SALES £ ——— ———	FINISH Miles — START Miles — TOTAL Miles —								
				EXPENSES — accommodation — meals — petrol etc TOTAL								£

Control ratios such as:
   Orders/Interviews =
   Interviews/Calls =
   £ Order value/£ Travelling cost =
can be calculated.

*   Name/Town
**   Sales call   C
       Sales interview   I
       Telephone interview   T
       Visit   V
***   Products by reference number
****   Miscellaneous, eg Order gained from
                               Order lost to
*****   Weekly and monthly figures may be carried forward

Customer control

A customer record should exist for all major customers upon whom regular sales calls are to be made. A specimen is shown below.

Customer record						
ACCOUNT				PHONE		
CONTACT				Best Time/Day/Month		
BUSINESS TYPE				POTENTIAL SALES £ / year		
Date	Payment status*	Objectives**	Results	Order value	Products	Objections***

* Checked prior evening
** Write objectives for next call to this customer immediately after sales call
*** For future interview planning

Channels of distributions

How will your goods reach the end user?

What channels of distribution do your competitors use?

Use this map to identify the best channels for your products to reach the end user.

| 1st tier manufacturer |

    Primary manufacturer

        Processor

           Importer

| 2nd tier manufacturer |

    Assembler

        Converter

           Finisher

| Middleman |

    Factor

      Wholesaler

        Distributor

          Agent

| Retail |

    Mail order
     Catalogue
      Party plan
       Franchise
        Sales agent
         Fairs/exhibitions
         Market stall
          Specialist shop
           Independent shop
          Multiple shop
         Supermarket

| END USER |

How do your chosen channels influence your:

- Prices?
- Discounts?
- Advertising?

Forecasting sales

The firm which cannot generate a *sales forecast* has no reason to be in business. Nevertheless sales forecasting is not easy, nor is it always accurate. Here are five ways in which your sales can be predicted. Use one or more methods.

1. Customers x orders

Average size of sales transaction	x	Customers		Sales £
£	x	/day /week /month /year	=	/day /week /month /year

Take seasonal factors into account.

2. Product/customer matrix

Customer	Z	Y	X	W	V
Product					
A					
B					
C					
D					
E					
Customer totals £					

Product totals

£

_____
_____
_____
_____
_____
_____

GRAND TOTAL

NB. In many businesses 80 per cent of sales will come from 20 per cent of products/customers

Have you asked your customers about their buying plans?

3. Extrapolation of present trends

	Actual				Forecast growth	
Annual sales	1982	1983	1984	1985	1986	1987
Divided by annual sales	÷	÷	÷	÷		
in previous year	1981	1982	1983	1984		
∴ Annual growth =	%	%	%	%	%	%

1986 Sales forecast =
1987 Sales forecast =

4. 'Z' charts

The trend of moving annual total sales (= sales in last 12 months) will suggest future levels of sales. Intermediate sales targets can also be set. The example shows seasonal sales to December.

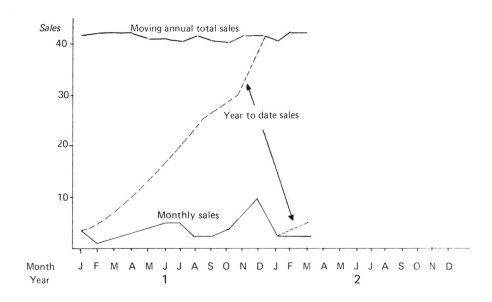

5. Market share

Year	Total market in units (a)	Competitors' market share %					Your company share % (b)	Your sales units (a)x(b)	Your selling price £/unit	Sales forecast £
		A	B	C	D	E				
1983										
1984										
1985										
1986										
1987										

Now check:

	£	Units
Sales forecasts		
Production capacity		

The marketing plan for bigger businesses

For larger start-ups and major expansions, a written detailed marketing plan is desirable. Financiers may wish to see it incorporated into your business plan.

The marketing plan is the blueprint for marketing action and the document used for monitoring performance to show whether marketing objectives are being achieved. There are a number of possible formats in common use; this is one variation.

1. *Introduction and background*
   Assessment of market potential: market research information.
   Analysis of Strengths, Weaknesses, Opportunities, Trends: (SWOT analysis).
   Analysis of competitive situation: existing market shares, competitions, marketing strategies; possible counter moves, other likely reaction.
   Examination of human resources: key personnel, their responsibilities and potential.

2. *Marketing strategy outline*
   Existing products: are they in growth, maturity, decline?
   Proposed new products: pre-launch/launch planning, investment plans.
   Written statements summarising product attributes: the brand propositions or brand intentions.
   Features/Benefits analysis: key consumer benefits and competitive comparisons — Unique Selling Proposition (USP).
   Proposed pricing strategy: what will the market stand?
   Proposed distribution strategy: manufacturing/warehousing facilities, locations and costs.

3. *Strategic objectives. Where are we going?*
   What targets, benchmarks of achievement do we set ourselves?
   Are these detailed, specific and measurable?
   Are they relevant, clearly understandable, challenging/demanding but achievable?
   Marketing action plans to achieve above objectives, resources required and their deployment.

4. *Marketing monitoring and control*
   Detailed breakdown of action plan (in 3 above) with monitoring methods.

Sales projections			Sales territory	
Profit projections	Broken		Product	— 1 year firm
Market shares/penetration	down by		Key market	— 2 years indicative
Selling expense			Major accounts	

   Sales operating budgets detailing each of the above features with projected attainment levels for each of the designated accounting/trading periods (usually monthly, sometimes quarterly/weekly).

5. *Physical stock levels at key dates*
   To meet seasonal variations permitting steady production with minimum inventory levels.

6. *Marketing support activities* needed to achieve the proposed objectives, eg:

   Sales training programmes
   Recruitment of additional personnel — job descriptions
   Advertising/sales promotion agency briefs
   Market research briefs etc.

7. *Longer term strategic objectives*

   Research and development
   New product developments
   New market development
   Diversifications etc.

   For many projects, the marketing plan is an important component in an overall business plan.

Chapter 5

Now I Need the Cash...

Sources of finance

The sources of finance are basically few in number. The list is properly headed by: self, family and friends.

1. **Self, family and friends**

   Loans and equity

2. **Shareholders and directors**

   Loans and equity

3. **Internal company sources** (not applicable to start-ups)

   Retained profits, cash collection, stocks and creditors

4. **Clearing banks**

   Overdraft, short-, medium- and long-term loans, Loan Guarantee Scheme
   Also some start-up and equity packages
   (Some building societies will provide long-term business development loans.)

5. **Second-tier finance**

   Hire purchase, leasing, contract hire, sale and leaseback, factoring and invoice discounting (see pages 58-9).

6. **Specialist financial institutions**

   Merchant banks and Investors in Industry Group (formerly ICFC)
   British Technology Group
   Pension funds
   Investment trusts
   Insurance companies

   Plus: Banks other than clearing banks
   Some local authorities, development corporations and enterprise boards

7. **Venture development capital**

   Venture capital funds
   Business Expansion Scheme funds (equity only)
   Private investors

8. **Mergers and acqusitions**

9. **Grants**

   Government and local authority
   Trusts: Prince's, Royal Jubilee, Youth Enterprise Scheme

10. **Money lenders**

    Mentioned for the sake of completeness only, and not to be used in business.

How much have 'Self, family and friends' provided?   £

What proportion of total start-up funds does this come to?   %

Second tier finance

Brief descriptions of additional financing options are given below. Professional advice from your accountant should clarify which, if any, would suit the business best.

Hire purchase

- Outright ownership of the equipment at the end of the hire period.
- Capital allowances and other grants may be claimed at the outset by the hirer.
- Hire purchase usually requires a deposit, and hire payments comprise capital and interest — only the interest element is tax deductible.

Lease purchase

- Where no deposit is payable by the hirer, the agreement may be called lease purchase.

Leasing (sometimes referred to as tax or finance leases)

- Capital allowances and grants are held by the leasing company, and in some measure passed on as reduced rentals.
- At the end of the lease period, a secondary period of lease may be taken up as an option at a nominal rental. Alternatively, the equipment may be purchased via a third party with drawback to the lessee.
- Lease rentals are treated as expenses, and therefore deductible against tax.
- Closed end leases run for a fixed term of one to five years. Open ended leases can be terminated at any time after the nominated minimum period. Balloon leases allow part of the capital payment to be made at the end of the lease agreement.

Contract hire (operating leases)

- Differs from finance leases in that the lessor is responsible for maintenance and, if necessary, replacement of the asset. Useful where the term of the lease is short when compared to the life of the assets.

Sale and leaseback

- An agreement between the seller and lessor wherein the seller undertakes to take a lease on the equipment, usually properties or large capital asset, for an agreed and long-term period. It releases cash for more profitable investment elsewhere but reduces the security in the business.
- An agreement between a firm and an institution wherein the firm sells its property, or a large item of equipment, to the institution, and at the same time takes out a long-term lease on it for the institution.
- Releases capital for use in the business. Tax aspects need watching.

Summary

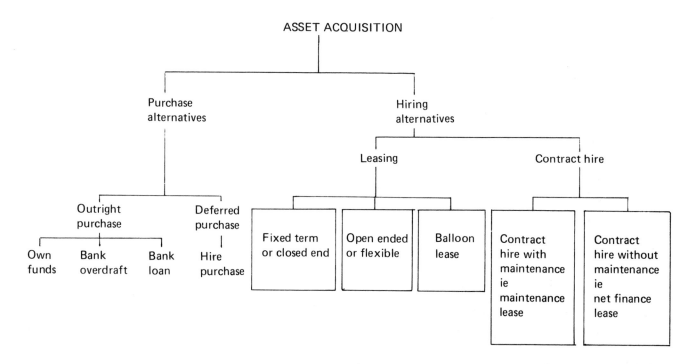

Factoring and invoice discounting

These two similar services may be used to bring a one-off improvement to cash flow.

Factoring

Factoring is selling your business debts to the factoring company on a continuing basis in order to obtain immediate cash payments in place of the expected future payments. The factoring service includes sales ledger, invoicing, insurance, cash collection and credit control systems.

Advantages	*Disadvantages*
Suits growth companies	Expensive — usually involves interest and service charges
Avoids extension of overdraft	More difficult for a young business to get accepted
Reduces administration	Concern about effect on customers
Reduces bad debts*	
Efficient paperwork	

* Non-recourse factoring

Invoice discounting

A simple service which makes cash advances against some or all sales invoices.

Advantages	*Disadvantages*
Cheaper than factoring	Needs well rated invoices
Customer relations unaffected	No help with sales administration
Suits growth companies	Expensive — usually involves interest and service charges
Avoids extension of overdraft	More difficult for a young business to get accepted by the
Reduces bad debts*	finance house

* Non-recourse invoice discounting

The Association of British Factors, Moor House, London Wall, London EC2Y 5HE; telephone 01-638 4090, and the Association of Invoice Factors, 109-113 Royal Avenue, Belfast BT1 1FF; telephone 0232 24522, exist to help their members and to control standards within the industry.

Equipment leasing

For smaller businesses the place of leasing in the mix of financial opportunities is not always clear.

Advantages	*Disadvantages*
Reduces capital need for start-up or expansion	Expensive
Off balance sheet, therefore leaves balance sheet ratios unaffected	Restrictions on use of equipment and, for cars, a limit on tax relief
Quick, often easy, to arrange	Medium-term inflexible contract
Stable facility, cannot be withdrawn	Asset now owned by user
'Full service' or flexible leasing options	Tax credits, if applicable, taken by lessor
Tax advantage to sole trader or partnership in first trading period	
Useful when equipment with only limited life needed, say three to five years, where capital could best be deployed for more long term use	

Before completing a lease agreement:

1. Understand nature of proposed agreement.
2. Check term, interest rate, inclusions, exclusions.
3. Note any method of residual valuation and payment.
4. Note trade-in and cancellation penalties.
5. Obtain cash flow and after-tax costs.

Matching finance

Money raised by a business should be matched to the purposes to which it is to be applied.

A common error is to use an overdraft facility to purchase plant and equipment.

This chart relates types, sources, and purposes of finance.

Type of finance	Purpose of finance	Suppliers of finance
Equity funding	Core finance Permanent capital	Self, family, shareholders, and retained profits Trusts* Private investors Development corporations and boards Venture capital funds Merchant banks Insurance companies Pension funds Business competitions
Short-term funding (0-3 year money)	Short-term working capital needs ● seasonal requirements ● bridging finance	Self, family, directors' loans and retained profits Debtors, stock reduction and extension of credit from suppliers Trusts* Clearing and other banks (overdraft) Merchant banks Finance houses Leasing companies Factoring and invoice discounting companies Money lenders
Medium-term funding (2-10 year money)	Medium-term assets ● plant and machinery Hard core working capital ● research and development	Self, family, directors' loans and retained profits Clearing and other banks (term loan and Loan Guarantee Scheme) Development corporations and boards Merchant banks Finance houses Leasing companies Central and local government loans and grants EEC loans
Long-term funding (10-25 year money)	Long-term assets ● land, buildings Corporate development	Self, family, directors' loans and retained profits Clearing and other banks Some building societies Development corporations and boards Merchant banks Finance houses Leasing companies Central and local government loans and grants EEC loans Insurance companies Pension funds

* Several trusts exist to provide money for start-ups, notably for the under 25 age group: Royal Jubilee and Prince's Trusts (including Youth Business Initiative), Youth Enterprise Scheme.

Cash required to start the business

The cash position is calculated in the forecasts for years 1 and 2 (see page 64). Without this calculation, there may be a tendency to underestimate the cash necessary to start the business.

It will be difficult to raise more than half the cash required to start the business from external sources, such as the bank.

This diagram shows the way cash flows out of, and later, we hope, back into a business. Its purpose is to encourage the calculation of the total cash needed to cover the worst cash position — this often occurs some months after start-up. When this figure is known, own cash 'o' and external cash 'x' from, say, the bank, may then be calculated.

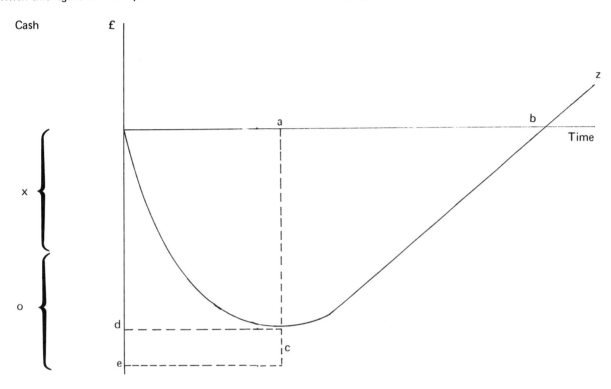

a = Time of worst cash position

b = Time of break-even on cash

c = Contingency — say 10 per cent of d

d = Worst cash position

e = c + d = *cash to start business*

o = Own finance (approximately equal to x)

x = External finance

z = Point at which second phase expansion may begin, often with a negative cash flow of its own.

Break-even point

As part of the start-up — and as part of the business plan — it is instructive to calculate the sales revenue necessary to break even against total costs.

Sales revenue	=	Units x price
Variable costs	=	Those costs which vary directly with throughput, eg raw materials
Fixed costs	=	Those costs which remain unchanged by throughput, eg rent
Total costs	=	Variable costs + fixed costs

The break-even graph often looks like this:

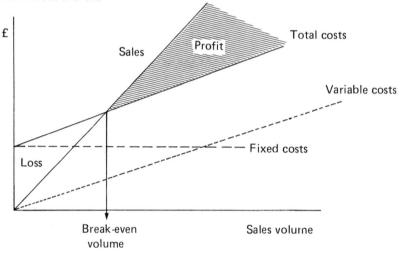

Now calculate:

$$\frac{\text{Break-even volume}}{\text{Production capacity}} \quad \text{x } 100 \quad = \quad \text{per cent}$$

$$\frac{\text{Break-even volume}}{\text{Current year sales target}} \quad \text{x } 100 \quad = \quad - \quad \text{per cent}$$

The higher these percentages, the less able the business is to withstand business uncertainty. Rethink when percentages exceed 70 per cent

$$\text{Gross margin \%} \quad = \quad \frac{\text{Sales revenue} - \text{variable cost}}{\text{Sales revenue}} \text{ x } 100$$

$$\text{Sales to break even} \quad = \quad \frac{\text{Fixed cost}}{\text{Gross margin}} \text{ x } 100$$

$$\text{Profit} \quad = \quad (\text{Sales revenue} - \text{sales to breakeven}) \text{ x } \frac{\text{Gross margin}}{100} \text{ (\%)}$$

The business plan

In an ideal world, the case presented to outside financial institutions should comprise the following. The proprietors also invest in the business; they too should have this information available.

1. *History of the business*
   A brief summary of the trading record and activities of the business since its inception, or during the last five years, whichever is the shorter. This paragraph would also include the numbers of employees through the period.
   List registered office, bankers, auditors/accountant, solicitor, and company registration numbers.

2. *Shareholders and senior managers*
   Include the major shareholders and their stakes. Describe the career details of the senior managers focusing on their successful track record throughout their careers.

3. *The market-place*
   Describe the market-place by, for example, geography, customers, business sector. Identify where possible total market potential, current existing market, and your target share of market.

   Examine major competitors in the major markets identified paying particular attention to their pricing and product improvement performance.

   Show the sales, marketing and distribution methods in use for the major parts of the business.

4. *Products and/or services*
   Describe the current range of products and services offered by the business, identifying the unique features and selling benefits associated with each one. Comment on the potential for *adding value* to existing products and services, and for developing totally new products and services.

5. *Business strategy (the five-year dream)*
   Write brief summary paragraphs that describe the overall business strategy, and the major functions of the business. These are likely to include capital structuring and financing, development, manufacturing, distribution, marketing relationships with suppliers, premises, equipment. Note also the future management structure.

6. *Shorter-term objectives*
   A brief list of the major problems and opportunities that the management intend to face and to take up during the forthcoming 12 months.

   This paragraph should include the major assumptions made about conditions which will affect the business.

7. *Management information system*
   A short demonstration of how major functions of the business are positively controlled by the existing management. Examples include credit control, research and development, cost control, purchase control, production cost control, cash flow control, sales control.

8. *Financial requirements*
   Tabular information designed to analyse the future financial requirements including the timing of intended expenditures, their sizes, the purpose of the expenditure and its planned benefit to the business.

   For larger projects, break-even levels of sales and sensitivity analyses would be helpful. (Computer packages used by professional accountants can produce these simply and effectively.) Include the contributions to the future cash requirements to be made by the shareholders and other sources of capital. Describe the repayment plans.

9. *Basic financial information*
   This should include the audited accounts for up to five years and the interim figures, ideally on a quarterly basis, for the current financial year. This should enable an up-to-date forecast for the current financial year to be made.

   For future periods, information should be presented to cover the operating budget and hence the cash flows for the next 12 months analysed at least by quarterly, and preferably by monthly, intervals. Outline budgets and cash flows for the following two years would also be most helpful. Summarise this information in the profit and loss accounts and balance sheets.

10. *Security*
    As a reserve document, not for immediate presentation, it is desirable to have available a summary of opportunities to provide personal security, business security, and the status of directors' loans.

    Also have available the Memorandum and Articles of Association, and Partnership Agreements, where applicable. Prepare for a visit by the financier to the premises.

Business forecasts

To help your accountant in the preparation of forecast cash flows, profit and loss accounts and balance sheets for the next three years, this basic data should be collected.

VAT status

VAT rate	%
VAT pay date	

Registration	Not required/Voluntary/Compulsory*
Industry	Exempt/Zero rated/Mixed/Fully rated*

* Delete as applicable

Financing

Equipment (if applicable)		Deposit		Advance		Repayments				Interest rate
Item	Cash cost £	Date payable	Size £	Date	Size £	Date of first	Frequency	Size £	Term months	% APR
Loan ...										
Hire purchase ...										
Leasing ...										

Current overdraft facility £ _____

Operating statistics

		Year 1	Year 2	Year 3
Stock cover at year end				
raw materials	days			
work in progress	days			
finished goods	days			
Gross margin	%			

		Year 1	Year 2	Year 3
Average time to collect debts	days			
Average time to pay suppliers	days			
Materials/sales	%			
Direct labour/sales	%			
Cash sales/total sales	%			

	Months												Year 1 Total		Quarters				Year 2 Total	Year 3 Total
	1	2	3	4	5	6	7	8	9	10	11	12			1	2	3	4		

	Pre start-up or last financial year end

Receipts

Proprietors'/shareholders' capital introduced
Directors'/shareholders' loans
Grants/other

Payments

Fixtures/fittings
Equipment

Note. Enter description and *either* amount paid when bought outright, *or* complete financing section above.

Now complete as much as possible of this form. With the exception of financing costs, write the figures on the basis of sales made and costs incurred (not as paid) and *exclusive of VAT*.

	Pre start-up or last financial year end	Months												Year 1 Total	Quarters				Year 2 Total	Year 3 Total
		1	2	3	4	5	6	7	8	9	10	11	12		1	2	3	4		
Sales																				
Direct materials																				
Year end stock*																				
Usage																				
Purchases pattern																				
NB. Total purchases for year = Closing stock + Usage − Opening stock. Purchases per period = Total purchases for the year spread according to purchase pattern.																				
Direct labour (inc NI)																				
Selling and distribution																				
Carriage																				
Packing																				
Advertising and promotion																				
Travel																				
Sales salaries (inc NI)																				
Sales commissions																				
Others																				
Occupation and administration																				
Rent																				
Rates																				
Post																				
Gas**																				
Electricity**																				
Water**																				
Printing and stationery																				
Insurances																				
Repairs and maintenance																				
Decoration and minor improvements																				
Telephone***																				
Professional fees																				
Bank charges																				
Salaries (inc NI)																				
Others																				
Financing costs (likely to be computed by your accountant)																				
Overdraft interest																				
Loan interest																				
Hire purchase/leasing charges																				

* Pre start-up or last year end figures only

** Include connection charges

*** Include connection, equipment, rentals and call costs.

Basic rules of bank lending

The clearing banks operate to simple lending rules. The business plan will recognise the rules and adapt to them.

1. *Equal contributions from the businessman and the bank*

   - the '£ for £' rule, *or*
   - shareholders'/proprietors' equity: borrowing = 1:1

2. *Full security on the bank's lending*
   Often provided by:

   - personal guarantees
   - land (including buildings)
   - stocks and shares
   - life assurance policies
   - business assets, eg debtors, stock, fixed assets.

   The bank requires the security to be easy to value, readily marketable and easy to obtain good legal title to.

   NB. The Loan Guarantee Scheme (LGS) now operates for some cases for which available security is insufficient to support the required loan, see page 68.

3. *Capacity to service interest charges*
   The degree to which planned profits exceed interest charges varies from bank to bank, but aim at a multiple of 4:1.

4. *Capability to repay the loan*
   The ability to repay within the term.

   The business plan will cover paragraphs 1 to 4 above and describe the nature of the proposition.

Finally, and probably most important:

5. *The borrower himself.*

   - his integrity and reliability
   - his capability of carrying out his business plan.

Presenting your case personally to the bank

The bank manager is required to make an assessment of you and your project. While the business plan will say much about the project, the presentation interview will be the best time to communicate your enthusiasm, commitment, and ability to manage. Use this 10 point checklist:

1. Complete the business plan. Include details according to the size of the finance package required.

2. Identify a 'preferred' list of bank branches with named managers, your own bank to head the list.

3. Personalise the front page and the summary of the plan to each of the 'preferred' list bank managers.

4. Make an appointment of a sensible duration with a manager of appropriate seniority, having regard to the size of the financial package requested.

5. Leave the business plan with the manager three to four days ahead of the appointment.

6. Plan out the main points you wish to stress during your introductory comments at the interview.

7. Arrive early for the appointment, appropriately dressed.

8. Make main points simply and quickly, and in so doing show how well you understand the market for your product or service.

9. Answer the manager's questions to amplify and support the written business plan in a way which will demonstrate your personal capability to run the business and your commitment to it.

10. Ask for the finance specified on front page (3 above).

The bank manager then has three responses:

Responses	*Your reaction*
1. Agree	Ask about costs, interest rate and conditions, obtain facility letter.
2. Want to think about it	Agree decision date, submit any further needed information.
3. Reject	Find out objections and try to agree a re-presentation date.

The government-backed Loan Guarantee Scheme (LGS)

In the absence of sufficient security, the major banks may use the LGS to help business start-ups and expansions[*] The money is expensive with a 5 per cent premium on the guaranteed element of the loan, but it can overcome some of the basic rules of bank lending (see page 66). See how it might work in the following small start-up. Then write in your own figures.

Typical start-up

	(% of sales)	First year of trade £000	Your forecasts for first year
Sales		20	
Gross margin	(50%)	10	
Profit (pre-tax, pre-interest, loan)	(10%)	2	
Fixed assets		5	
Equipment	4		
Vehicles	1		
Stock and debtors	(40%)[**]	8	
Creditors	(13%)[**]	3	

Two financing options
(examples only)

(a) Proprietor/Shareholders alone	£000	(b) Using Loan Guarantee Scheme (LGS)	£000
Investment, say	10	Overdraft @ 14% (secured)	5.0
		3-year guaranteed loan @ 16%	5.0
		∴ Overdraft interest	0.7
		Loan interest	0.7
		Loan premium	0.2
		Charge to P&L	1.6
Profit (pre-tax)	2	Profit (pre-tax)	0.4
		From which loan repayments of	1.4
		have to be made	

NB.   Proprietor's capital is cheap money.
      LGS does not cover overdraft finance.
      Interest and loan repayments can eliminate profits
      Business failure rates under LGS are said to be 40 per cent.
      Take advantage of monitoring and reporting required by the lender.

  [*] At the time of writing, the Loan Guarantee Scheme had not been extended beyond December 1985.
[**] See *The Genghis Khan Guide to Business*, Brian Warnes (Osmosis Publications Ltd)

Benefiting from government grants

Many grant aid programmes come under the general description of 'selective financial assistance' which, in turn, covers the Department of Trade and Industry's 'Support for Innovation' and 'Selective Assistance to Manufacturing Industry' packages.

While separate application forms tend to be applicable to each scheme, the following principles apply:

1. *The company*

    (a) Must be viable (but not too viable)
    (b) Must be well managed
    (c) Should be likely to succeed
    (d) Should contact Department of Trade and Industry. Try to get to know personally the officer responsible for the appraisal.

2. *The project*

    (a) Must be viable
    (b) Must have a clear end product
    (c) Must be additional in that one of the following apply:

    - without aid the project would be cancelled
    - with aid, the project would be changed beneficially
    - its time-scale would be accelerated
    - it would be enlarged

    (d) Should provide industrial and economic benefits
    (e) Must be innovatory, for 'Support for Innovation'
    (f) Must be approved *before any expenditure* is incurred.

NB. The approval process itself can also take several months, so there is a need to plan ahead if advantage is to be taken of government grant aid.

Regional Development Grants are available in certain localities. Details should be obtained from the Department of Trade and Industry, the Small Firms Service, or the Local Enterprise Agency.

Schemes and services available to small businesses

Local Enterprise Agencies, the Small Firms Service and accountants have more detailed information on schemes to benefit your business.

Which of these schemes may help your business?

Other possible schemes include:
MSC: Opentech, Pickup, Itecs
DTI: Enterprise zones
Colleges: Management training
Tourist boards:- Advice, grant and loan aid
CDA: co-operatives
EIEC: Workshops and industrial units

Schemes (column headings):
- Local Authority Grants and Finance
- Skillcentres
- Youth Training Scheme
- Training Grant Aid
- Recruitment and Training Package
- Training Consultancy
- Management Extension Programme
- New Enterprise Programme
- MSC Training courses/Seminars
- Export Project Grants
- Export Credits Guarantee
- Export Market Entry Help
- Export Advice
- EEC Grants (inc Business Improvement Schemes)
- EEC Loans
- Regional Development Grants
- Regional Selective Assistance
- Quality Assurance Projects
- New Technology Investment
- New Technology Implementation Studies
- Loan Guarantee Scheme
- Major Project Grants
- Support for Innovation
- New Technology Study Grants
- Products and process Consultancy
- COSIRA
- Local Enterprise Agencies
- Small Firms Service
- Business Expansion Scheme
- Enterprise Allowance Scheme

Row categories:

Starting up	
All firms	Nationwide / Assisted areas / Development areas / Closure areas / Rural
Manufacturing	Nationwide / Assisted areas / Development areas / Closure areas / Rural

Up to 200 employees	
All firms	Nationwide / Assisted areas / Development areas / Closure areas / Rural
Manufacturing	Nationwide / Assisted areas / Development areas / Closure areas / Rural

Up to 500 employees	
All firms	Nationwide / Assisted areas / Development areas / Closure areas
Manufacturing	Nationwide / Assisted areas / Development areas / Closure areas

70

Business information document

The Prevention of Fraud Act places the entrepreneur at risk of heavy damages when the public is canvassed for money other than by licensed dealers in securities, eg banks and brokers. When the time comes to seek additional investment in the business, summary information of the sort indicated below will determine the level of interest in the investor's side. An interested investor would subsequently expect a full business plan. It is important to seek professional advice before canvassing for finance. The rules are strict and must be observed.

Main activities

Main markets and competition

Product range

- Existing products
- New products
- Patent position

Management team

Number of employees

- Past
- Present
- Projected

Main shareholders

		Actual				Proposed		
		1982	1983	1984	1985	1986	1987	1988
Sales	£000							
Gross profit	£000							
Pre-tax profit	£000							
Balance sheet summary								
Issued capital								
Reserves								
Loans (with terms and security)								
Fixed assets								
Investments								
Current assets								
Current liabilities								
Cash requirements								
Capital expenditure								

...and Premises

Working from home

Home may be a most suitable first base for the starter business. Whether it is legal and practical is a matter of fact and degree — this checklist may prevent expensive mistakes.

Issue	Check with	Date done	Result
Planning permission Building regulations	Planning Department Local Authority		
Restrictive covenants ● Leasehold ● Freehold	Lease Agreement or Title Deed Solicitor		
Mortgage	Building Society		
Insurance	Insurance Company		
Tax consequences	Accountant		
Other legislation relevant to your business plans	Local Authority Solicitor		
Disturbance	Neighbours		
Effect on family life and social life	Family		
Your own work efficiency at home	Self		

If work at home is not practicable, it may be worth contacting your Borough, District or County Council, or your Local Enterprise Agency about managed workshops or nursery units. Such premises are specially designed for start-ups and young businesses.

Property requirements checklist

Before beginning the search, complete the 'Ideal' column describing the property really needed to see the business through its early years. Fill in notes for interesting properties seen. Try to find at least three properties which come near to meeting the ideal needs.

	Ideal	Property A	Property B	Property C
Type Warehouse Factory Office Shop				
Location/Town				
How Large? (in sq ft/metres) Warehouse Factory Office Shop				
Access Pedestrian Vehicles Loading				
Floor loading				
Height Access doors Storage space Working space				
Parking Essential Preferable Not important				
Facilities Office accommodation Heating Lighting Ventilation Mains services — gas — electricity — water — drainage — finishes/insulation — security — lift				
When available				

Costs
Purchase
Rent — Length of lease
    — Annual rent
    — Rent review
    — Premium
Rateable value
Legal (Vendor's costs)
Adaptation and moving costs				

Constraints Fire hazards Planning permission Security Refurbishing Restrictive covenants Future expansion Neighbours				
Check also the following points: Noise Vibration Smells Overshadowing by buildings, trees etc.				

Rent reviews

Rent reviews have become a fundamental aspect of nearly every modern lease on commercial and industrial property. Landlords are reluctant to grant leases with the rent fixed for a long period, and tenants, notwithstanding their statutory protection, are reluctant to forgo their security by accepting short leases.

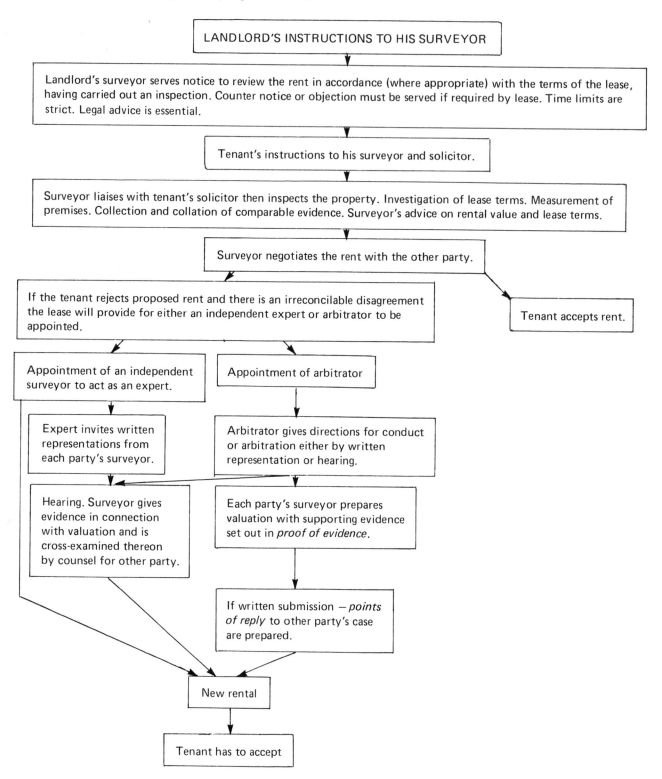

LANDLORD'S INSTRUCTIONS TO HIS SURVEYOR

Landlord's surveyor serves notice to review the rent in accordance (where appropriate) with the terms of the lease, having carried out an inspection. Counter notice or objection must be served if required by lease. Time limits are strict. Legal advice is essential.

Tenant's instructions to his surveyor and solicitor.

Surveyor liaises with tenant's solicitor then inspects the property. Investigation of lease terms. Measurement of premises. Collection and collation of comparable evidence. Surveyor's advice on rental value and lease terms.

Surveyor negotiates the rent with the other party.

Tenant accepts rent.

If the tenant rejects proposed rent and there is an irreconcilable disagreement the lease will provide for either an independent expert or arbitrator to be appointed.

Appointment of an independent surveyor to act as an expert.

Appointment of arbitrator

Expert invites written representations from each party's surveyor.

Arbitrator gives directions for conduct or arbitration either by written representation or hearing.

Hearing. Surveyor gives evidence in connection with valuation and is cross-examined thereon by counsel for other party.

Each party's surveyor prepares valuation with supporting evidence set out in *proof of evidence*.

If written submission — *points of reply* to other party's case are prepared.

New rental

Tenant has to accept

The complexities which normally prevail clearly require the experience and skills of professional advisers.

Lease renewals

In many cases, the expiration of a lease can have an effect similar to that of a rent review, in that the tenant may have been paying an historic rent, in which case the landlord will not have been receiving an economic return on his investment.

Upon the expiry of a lease the contractual commitment by both parties terminates, although the tenant usually has security of tenure under the provisions of the Landlord and Tenant Act 1954, supplemented by the Law of Property Act 1969; thus the relationship between the landlord and tenant will normally continue although the landlord may wish to exercise his statutory right to regain possession of the premises for the purpose of redevelopment of his own occupation, or one of the other statutory reasons.

This highly simplified chart describes the process of renewals.

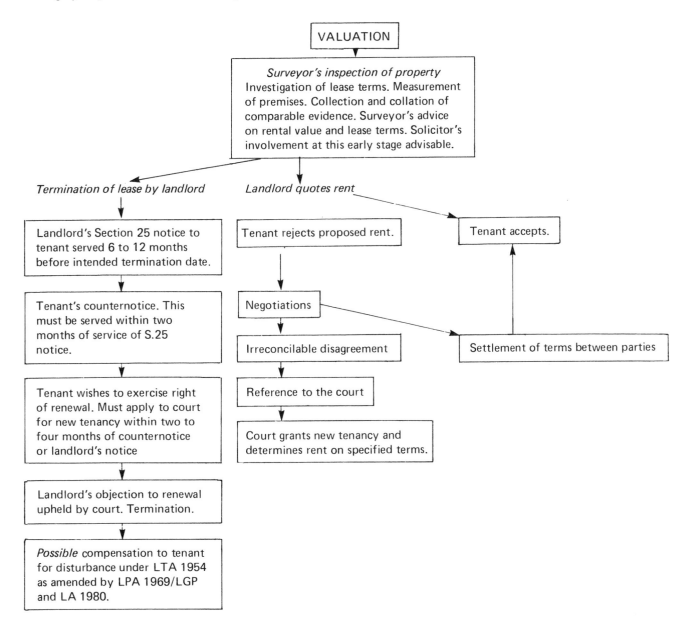

Whether one is landlord or tenant, it is essential to take professional advice at the earliest possible moment.

The costs of getting into premises

Most attention is given to rent and rates.

1st year costs

Rent: size	[ft²]	x	price	[£ /ft²]	£
Rates: poundage	[£ /£]	x	rateable value	[£]	£ _____
				TOTAL	£

But the total cost of getting into premises is *increased* by most of the factors listed below:

Other costs	Notes	Amount £
Advance rent	Often three months' rent	
Lease premium	Ask about reverse premium in a slack market	
Survey	Vital for full repairing lease	
Legal	Usually both landlord's and tenant's costs	
Insurances	See lease	
Property improvements	Some may be paid by landlord	
Property alterations	Permission required	
Planning permission	'Change of use' fees	
Services and service charges	3-phase electricity, gas, telephone, ventilation, caretaker, common areas. Who pays? How much?	
Security	Who provides? Who pays?	
Removal	Per quotation	
Disturbance to business	Usually underestimated	
Fire Environmental Health and Safety costs	} Check with relevant authorities	
May be aided by		
Moving-in package	Could include rent holiday, legal fees, improvements	

The routine of planning permission

Professional advice will be necessary to help you unravel the intricacies of planning permission. This flowchart has been designed as a much simplified pattern of planning permission routine.

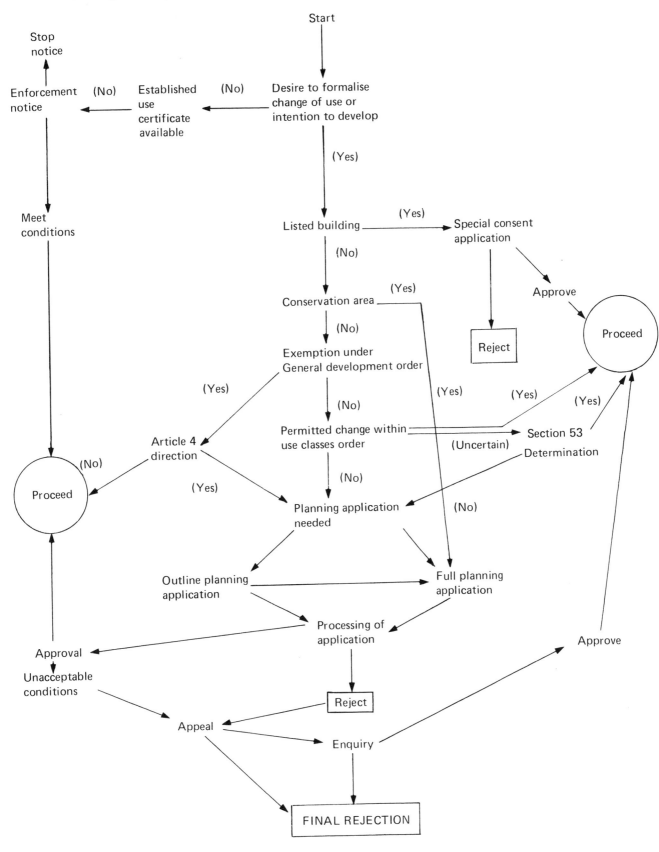

Watch out for opportunities in Special Planning Zones. See *Lifting the Burden on Business*, HMSO, 1985.

A guide to planning applications for commerce and industry

Applications, with appropriate fees, should be made to the Chief Planning Officer, Borough or District Council, for permission to develop land. Applications are needed for new buildings and the change of use of existing buildings or other land.

The checklists below give a quick guide to the information which will generally be required, as a minimum, as part of the planning application. Basically there are two types of planning application, both of which are best done under professional guidance and should be discussed informally with an officer from the Planning Department *before* an application is made.

A. Outline application

An outline application can only be made for the erection of new buildings (or extensions to existing buildings). This will probably be appropriate in cases where it is initially necessary or advisable to establish the *principle* of new industrial development. This will be on land *not* in an industrial area or *not* allocated for industrial use in the local district plans.

An outline application needs:

1. Four completed copies of forms P1 and P1A.
2. Four paper copies of a plan (preferably to a 1:2500 or 1:1250 scale) indicating the land in question within a red edge and any other land owned or controlled edged blue.
3. Any explanatory material which the applicant may wish to give, or which the local planning authority may require.

An outline permission granted will require the submission of a further application (a reserved matters application) giving full details of the new development.

B. Full (detailed) application

A detailed application needs:

1. Four completed copies of forms P1 and P1A.
2. Four paper copies of plans showing:

   (a) The area of land in question within a red edge.
   (b) Plans and elevations of the proposed building(s), including details of materials and finishes.
   (c) Details of the treatment of the remainder of the site, including size, location and surfacing of:

       (i) car parking areas
       (ii) loading, unloading and manoeuvring space
       (iii) open storage space (if any) and details of any proposed screening.

   (d) Details of existing trees together with a proposed landscaping scheme.

Applications will also probably be required under the Building Regulations and an officer in the Planning Department will be pleased to provide advice on this aspect.

Local district or borough plans are available from the Chief Planning Officer, at the council offices.

Change of use: Is planning permission necessary?

The Town and Country Planning (Use Classes) Order 1972 sets out 18 use classes which cover the use of land and buildings. Changes of use within a defined class do not require planning permission. Changes of use *between* use classes, or to or from other uses which do not fall within any of the 18 categories generally require planning permission. However, the Town and Country Planning General Development Orders 1977 to 1981 allow the following *exceptions:*

(a) From any of the following special shops to an ordinary shop:

 (i) Shop for the sale of hot food
 (ii) Tripe shop
 (iii) Shop for the sale of pet animals or birds
 (iv) Cats' meat shop
 (v) Shop for the sale of motor vehicles.

 NB. The change of use of a shop *to* any of these special shops *does* require planning permission.

(b) From Class 4 (General Industrial) to Class 3 (Light Industrial).
(c) From Class 3 or Class 4 to Class 10 (Warehousing).
(d) From Class 10 to Class 3.

In the case of (c) and (d), there is a limit of 235 square metres; over and above this figure planning permission is required.

The Use Classes Order defines a number of terms including 'shop', 'office', 'industrial building', 'light industrial building' and 'general industrial building'. The specified classes should not be stretched to include activities which do not clearly fall within them; unusual activities must be considered as separate uses in themselves. Changes of use to and from any such individual uses will generally require planning permission.

If you are in any doubt about the use class into which your activity falls, or whether planning permission is required for your use of a particular site or building, contact the Borough or District Council Planning Department which will be pleased to advise you.

Eighteen categories of use classes

Class

1. Shop, except for sale of

 (i) hot food
 (ii) tripe shop
 (iii) pet animals or birds
 (iv) cats' meat shop
 (v) motor vehicles

2. Use as an office for any purpose
3. Use as a light industrial building for any purpose
4. Use as a general industrial building for any purpose
5. (Special Industrial Group A). Alkali & Works Regulation Act 1906(a), which is not included in any of Classes 6, 7, 8 or 9
6. (Special Industrial Group B). Processes, carried on in or adjacent to a quarry or mine
7. (Special Industrial Group C). Processes based on the treatment of mineral except as an ancillary to the extraction itself.
8. (Special Industrial Group D). Use for any of the following purposes:

 (i) oils
 (ii) cellulose
 (iii) linseed oil
 (iv) hot pitch or bitumen
 (v) stoving
 (vi) production contains organic chemicals
 (vii) rubber from scrap
 (viii) chlorphenols or chlorcresols

9. (Special Industrial Group E). Listed industries, businesses or trades
10. Wholesale warehouse or repository for any other purpose
11. Boarding or guest house, or an hotel
12. A residential or boarding school or college
13. Public worship or religious instruction
14. Children, old people or persons under disability, or in a convalescent home, a nursing home, a sanatorium or a hospital
15. Health centre, a school treatment centre, a clinic, a crèche, a day nursery or a dispensary, consulting room or surgery
16. Art gallery, a museum, public library or reading room, public hall, exhibition hall
17. Theatre, cinema, music hall or concert hall
18. Dance hall, skating rink, swimming bath, Turkish or foam bath, gymnasium or sports hall.

Chapter 7

Legal and Tax Matters

Legal format at start-up

The common view is that the 'sole trader' formula is preferable at lower levels of taxable profits. But there is no 'right' answer, and the decision ought to be made on the basis of what best meets the current and foreseeable business needs. Your solicitor or your accountant can help you to make the decision.

Sole trader

Advantages

No legal formalities
Total responsibility
Short-term tax benefits
Taxed as individual
Financial flexibility
May start at any time
Ease of winding up
Self-employed pension facility

Disadvantages

Personal assets at disposal of creditors
Capital Gains Tax on goodwill when you incorporate — subject to deferment
Capital and stamp duties when you incorporate
No corporate pension provision
Loss of some social security benefits

Partnership

As for sole trader plus:

Advantages

Single tax assessment

Disadvantages

Partnership agreement advisable
Difficult to grow through gaining new partners
Each partner responsible for all debts

Limited companies

Advantages

Limited liability*
Lower tax burden at higher profit levels
Company tax burden at higher profit levels
Company pension schemes
Status/Image
May be easier to sell shares depending on initial structure
Loans and shareholders easily added to corporate structure
Employee status for social security benefits

* May be negated in practice by guarantees

Disadvantages

Can be costly to establish
Trading allowed only after incorporation
Loss of profit sharing flexibility
Formal company meetings
Filing of audited accounts
Higher professional fees
No loans to directors
Schedule E taxation for directors
All employees on PAYE
Corporation Tax liability

Co-operative

Owned and controlled by those working in it
   — membership usually open to all employees subject to qualifications laid down by the members.
   — one member, one vote irrespective of individual shareholdings.
Profits shared in proportion to work, therefore no capital gain.
Members can organise business to suit their own objectives, rather than those of an owner or boss.
Usually registered as either an Industrial and Provident Society or company limited by guarantee.

INDUSTRIAL AND PROVIDENT SOCIETY

Advantages	*Disadvantages*
Model rules for ease of registration	Shareholding limited to £10,000 per member
Simpler rules and reporting requirements than companies	Difficult to attract outside risk capital
Shares easily repurchased by society when a member leaves	Share value remains at £1 each
Bonus on profits and loan interest paid without deduction of tax	Formal company meetings
Special Corporation Tax rate	Filing of audited accounts
Registrar will advise individual societies	All employees on PAYE
Tax relief on loans used for investing in society	Corporation Tax liability
Company pension scheme	Minimum of seven members
Exemption from 'close company' provisions	Not universally understood by accountants, solicitors and bank managers
No directors: management committee elected by members	Not eligible for Business Expansion Scheme funds
Organised for the benefit of members who work in the business	Cannot issue bonus shares free of tax
No filing fee for annual return	Limited interest only paid on shares
	Higher registration cost than company

COMPANY LIMITED BY GUARANTEE

Advantages	*Disadvantages*
Model rules for ease of registration	No share capital
Can be formed with only two members	Difficult to attract outside risk capital
Easy to join, easy to leave	Formal company meetings
Company pension scheme	Filing of audited accounts
Registered under Companies Act and widely understood by accountants, solicitors etc	All employees on PAYE
Possible to obtain charitable status	Not eligible for Business Expansion Scheme funds
Constitution may be drafted with more flexibility	
Tax relief on loans for investing in company	
Organised for benefit of members who work in the business	

Note: Can sometimes be registered as a limited company with shares, but rules are often complex.

Partnerships

Unfortunately a number of business partnerships have difficulties due to the *absence* of a formal partnership agreement.

A partnership agreement drawn up with your accountant's and solicitor's help before the business begins should consider:

1. Members of the partnership
2. Period of the partnership: commencement, duration and termination
3. Name of the partnership
4. Business activities and location
5. Partnership premises including tenancy agreements/leases
6. Capital: sharing and interest thereon
7. Goodwill
8. Profit (and loss) sharing formula
9. Drawings on account of shares of profits
10. Treatment of remuneration, eg partners' fees and legacies from clients of the firm
11. Books of account
12. Annual accounts including accounting date
13. Clients' monies, if applicable
14. Accountants
15. Bankers
16. Responsibilities of partners including holiday entitlement
17. Negative covenants
18. Motor cars
19. Outgoing partners' arrangements
20. Compulsory retirement at given age
21. Admission of new partners
22. Pensions, annuities and insurance arrangements
23. Tax provisions and continuation election
24. Covenants in restraint of trade
25. Dissolution of partnership
26. Expulsion of partners
27. Serving of notices
28. Partnership meetings and voting thereat
29. Arbitration.

Business names

The name a business uses can be a great help to the business but there are a few constraints on the freedom of choice.

Sole trader

1. The individual's own name brings no extra requirements, eg Smith, J Smith.
2. A different name requires:

   - Letterheads, orders, invoices, receipts, payment demands to bear name and address of owner
   - A notice of the name and address to be prominently displayed in all business premises
   - An answer, in writing, to any request for owner's name and address.

Partnership

As above, except for partnerships of more than 20 persons for which additional regulations apply.

Limited companies

Subject to the approval of the Registrar of Companies, with requirements to avoid:

- The same name as another company
- Criminal or offensive names
- Names reserved by statute
- Names used by certain qualifying entities (eg bank)
- Names connected with the government.

There is also a statutory list of words for the use of which prior approval must be obtained.

Formation of limited companies

For some people it may be desirable to form a limited company at the time of start-up. For others, successful expansion may prompt professional advisers to suggest incorporation (formation of a limited company).

1. *Memorandum of Association* sets out:

    (a) Company name
    (b) Whether the registered office is in England, Wales, Scotland or Northern Ireland
    (c) The company's objects
    (d) A statement of the shareholders' liability
    (e) The number of authorised shares by type.

2. *Articles of Association* typically set out:

    (a) The procedure for calling general and extraordinary meetings
    (b) The responsibilities and rights of directors
    (c) Procedure for election of directors
    (d) The company's borrowing policies
    (e) Control of shares.

    A set of model Articles is usually available from accountants and solicitors incorporating the various provisions required by the Companies Acts.

3. *Declaration of Compliance*
    States that the directors have complied with Companies Acts.

Your solicitor and accountant will help you with:

Accounting reference date	Form 2
Share allotment	Form PUC2
Notification of registered office	Form 4a
Notification of new directors	Form 9b

Following the submission of these documents by your accountant or solicitor to the Registrar of Companies, and his acceptance, the Certificate of Incorporation will be issued. The Certificate and registration date should be displayed on public view, while the registration number and other formal details must appear on official company stationery.

Responsibilities of company directors

Many people see the position of being a company director through rose-coloured glasses, and as a status symbol. The responsibilities of being a company director, some of which are given below, should encourage you to discuss your individual case with your solicitor or accountant.

- Directors have to attend board meetings.
- They have to disclose their private interests and shares in the company.
- Directors must act with diligence and honesty, and know what is going on.
- They are liable for all debts of the company if, knowingly insolvent, they allow the company to trade into further debt.

Furthermore, there are these constraints on company directors:

- By the Articles of Association, directors are granted powers which may not be exceeded.
- They are elected and may be removed.
- They are subject to special requirements by the Inland Revenue with regard to expenses and perquisites.
- Normally, directors may not borrow money from the company.

Value added tax (VAT)

VAT is collected by HM Customs & Excise. Most businesses have to learn to live with it.

1. *Reasons for registering*
   Compulsory when turnover reaches the VAT threshold.
   High input VAT paid, which is recoverable.
   Credibility with other traders.
   NB. VAT registered customers can claim back invoiced VAT.

2. *Method of registering*
   Discuss with your accountant first.
   Identify VAT trade classification from VAT41 booklet.
   Read 'Should I be Registered for VAT?' (ref 700/1/83) and 'The Ins and Outs of VAT' (ref 700/15/83).
   Fill in form VAT 1. Send to local VAT office.
   Telephone VAT office for your number.
   Obtain any special leaflets relating to your industry.

3. *Operating the scheme*
   Read 'Filling in Your VAT Return' (ref 700/12/81).
   Maintain up-to-date, accurate books — see your accountant.
   Prepare to be inspected by an officer of HM Customs & Excise.
   Include VAT payments/receipts in cash flow projections.
   Keep all invoices as evidence of VAT payments.

4. *Remember*
   VAT on bad debts is recoverable only on proof of liquidation.
   VAT on entertaining of UK business people may not be claimed.
   VAT is not charged on second-hand car sales except when the car is sold for more than you paid for it.

HM Customs & Excise have available a comprehensive VAT Information Pack; contact your local office.

VAT groups and thresholds

This table enables areas of possible VAT liabilities to be reviewed.

Group	Exempt goods and services A	Zero-rated goods and services B	Standard 15 per cent rate C
1.	Land	Food	All goods and services not in columns A and B for VAT registered businesses.
2.	Insurance	Sewerage water	
3.	Postal	Books	
4.	Betting	Books, radio to the handicapped	
5.	Finance	News services	
6.	Education	Fuel and power	
7.	Health	Certain types of construction	
8.	Burial and cremation	International services	
9.	Professional bodies	Transport	
10.	Sporting competitions	Caravans, houseboats	
11.	Certain types of construction	Gold	
12.		Bank notes	
13.		Medicines and appliances	
14.		Exports	
15.		Charities	
16.		Children's clothing and footwear	

VAT is compulsory when turnover from columns B and C above reaches either the currently prescribed annual or quarterly figures. HM Customs & Excise must be notified within ten days of the end of the quarter in which taxable turnover exceeds the prescribed limits for the first time. Registration takes effect from the twenty-first day after the end of that quarter, or such earlier date as may be mutually agreed.

HM Customs & Excise are usually most helpful when queries and uncertainties are put to them.

Tax and the newly self-employed

The tax that you pay for the first *three* tax years that you are in business is normally based on the profits of your *first year alone*. Therefore, with careful planning, you may be able to minimise your tax bills in your early years to your considerable advantage. It is important that you discuss with your accountant as soon as possible how this is best achieved.

At the same time, your accountant should advise you on the best date to which your annual accounts should be prepared so as to delay your tax payments as much as possible, thus maximising your cash flow.

As an *employee*, your income tax and National Insurance contributions were deducted from your remuneration before you received it: that is, you could spend what you received. Now that you are self-employed, your annual income tax and Class 4 National Insurance contributions will normally be payable in two halves: the first half on 1 January in the tax year, and the second half six months later, on 1 July.

Furthermore, your income tax and Class 4 National Insurance bills for the first two or even three tax years are likely to land in your lap together when you least expect them, with only a few days before payment has to be made. You must therefore find out from your accountant what your liabilities are likely to be, and when you might have to pay them.

● It is essential that your cash forecast takes account of your income tax and National Insurance payments so that the cash is there when needed.

Business insurance

In addition to the insurance that an individual will take out in his private life, there is a need for the businessman to consider seriously the insurance he will need at business start-up, and then throughout his business career. The following list is designed to help him decide which to take out, and when.

	Immediate cover (date)	To be covered by (date)	Not relevant in foreseeable future
1. Fire and special perils			
2. Advance and consequential loss following fire, special perils, sprinkler damage, and machinery breakdown			
3. Burglary			
4. Employer's liability			
5. Professional indemnity			
6. Directors' and Officers' liability			
7. Public and product liability			
8. Money			
9. Commercial vehicles			
10. Goods in transit			
11. Private cars			
12. Mobile plant			
13. Contractors all risks			
14. Engineering — lifting equipment, electrical plant boilers, and general equipment			
15. Plate glass			
16. Key man (including personal accident and sickness, private hospital costs), group personnel			
17. Life assurance and pensions			
18. Computer and computer records			
19. Legal costs and expenses			
20. Livestock			
21. Marine and aircraft insurance			
22. Political risk			
23. Credit insurance			
24. Fidelity			

Which of these covers are you *required by law* to take out?

Licences and permissions

A wide variety of laws and regulations control and limit certain types of businesses. An indication of licences in which you could be involved follows:

Legislation	*Covering*	
Consumer Credit Act 1974	Credit sales Dealing in securities	
Transport Act 1983	Operators' licences	
Medicines Act 1968	Human and veterinary medicines	
Solicitors' Act 1974		
Veterinary Surgeons Act 1966 and similar Acts	Practice in certain professions	Professional advice from your solicitor is recommended
Registered Homes Act 1984	Nursing homes	
Betting, Gaming and Lotteries Act 1963	Gambling and gaming	
Employment Agencies Act 1973	Employment agencies	
Children's Act 1975	Employment of children	
Town & Country Planning Acts 1963-84	Planning permission	

The local Borough or District Council handles planning permission, and a range of other licences such as:

Music and dancing

Late night refreshments

Cinema

Theatre employers

Theatre performance of plays

Pleasure boats

Lotteries and amusements

Amusements with prizes

Food and ice cream

Hawkers

Street and house-to-house collections

Petroleum and paint storage

Private hire vehicle operator

Private hire and hackney carriage driver's licence

Private hire and hackney carriage vehicle licence

Pet shop

Breeding of dogs

Boarding of dogs

Riding establishments

Slaughterman

Dealing in game

Scrap metal dealing

Explosives and fireworks

Shops and factories

Make first contact with the Planning Department or Environmental Health Department.

For public houses, licensed restaurants, hotels, boarding houses and wine bars, contact the Justices' Clerk.

Then there are optional — but often desirable — licences: ABTA for travel agents, and industry codes of practice, eg National Inspection Council for Electrical Installation Contracting, National Association of Funeral Directors.

Data protection

The Data Protection Act 1985 requires any business that keeps records of personal data on individuals in computer files to register with the government. Existing data files should be registered in a six-month period beginning 11 November 1985. From 1986 new computerised records may need immediate registration. Further information is available from the Office of the Data Protection Registrar, Springfield House, Water Lane, Wilmslow, Cheshire SK9 5AX; telephone Wilmslow 535711.

Obtaining UK registered design protection

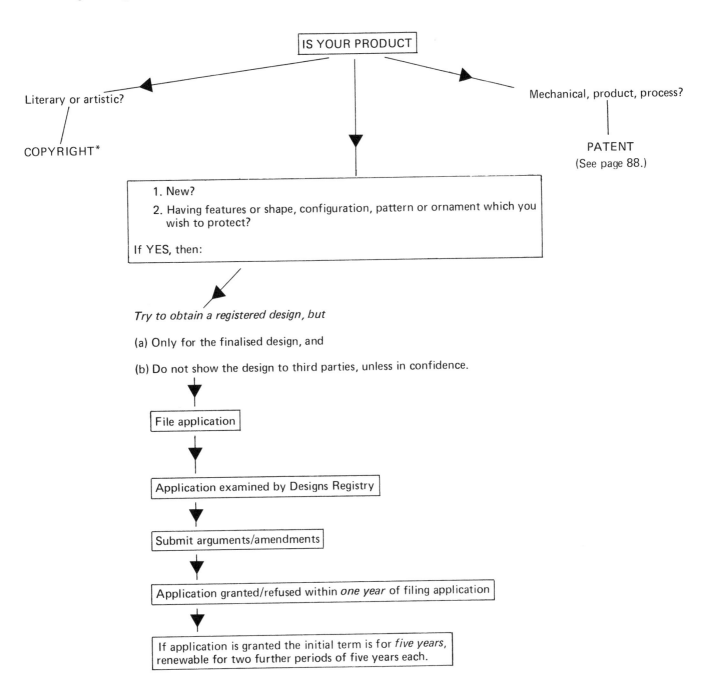

IS YOUR PRODUCT

Literary or artistic?

COPYRIGHT*

Mechanical, product, process?

PATENT
(See page 88.)

1. New?
2. Having features or shape, configuration, pattern or ornament which you wish to protect?

If YES, then:

Try to obtain a registered design, but

(a) Only for the finalised design, and

(b) Do not show the design to third parties, unless in confidence.

File application

Application examined by Designs Registry

Submit arguments/amendments

Application granted/refused within *one year* of filing application

If application is granted the initial term is for *five years*, renewable for two further periods of five years each.

*In many cases products of an original design are protected from illicit copying by the Design Copyright Act. This protection is inherent and immediate.

Professional advice at an early stage will help you to assess the value and chances of obtaining design registration. Please see also the free official pamphlet 'Protection of Industrial Designs', available from HM Stationery Office and the Patent Office, State House, 66-71 High Holborn, London WC1R 4TP.

Obtaining a UK patent

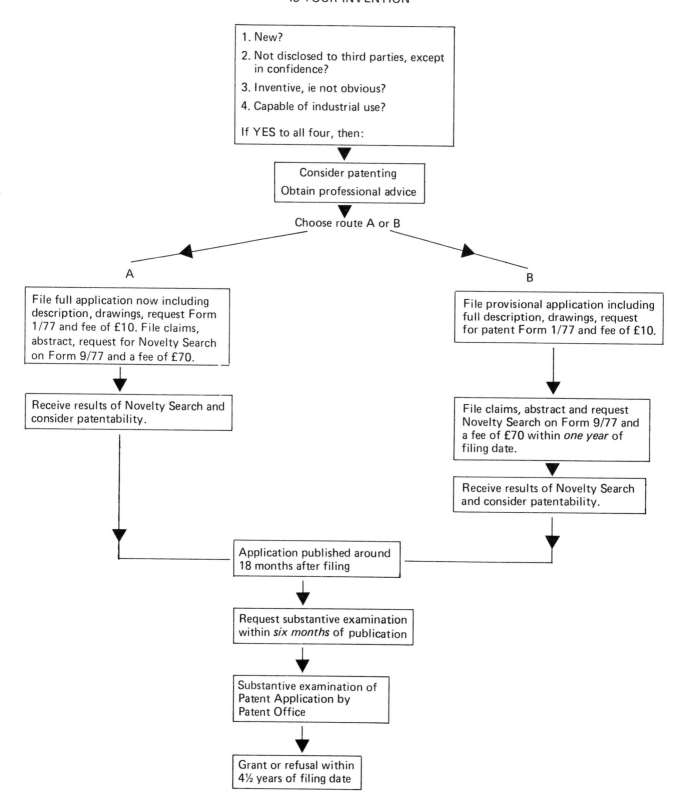

IS YOUR INVENTION

1. New?

2. Not disclosed to third parties, except in confidence?

3. Inventive, ie not obvious?

4. Capable of industrial use?

If YES to all four, then:

Consider patenting
Obtain professional advice

Choose route A or B

A

File full application now including description, drawings, request Form 1/77 and fee of £10. File claims, abstract, request for Novelty Search on Form 9/77 and a fee of £70.

Receive results of Novelty Search and consider patentability.

B

File provisional application including full description, drawings, request for patent Form 1/77 and fee of £10.

File claims, abstract and request Novelty Search on Form 9/77 and a fee of £70 within *one year* of filing date.

Receive results of Novelty Search and consider patentability.

Application published around 18 months after filing

Request substantive examination within *six months* of publication

Substantive examination of Patent Application by Patent Office

Grant or refusal within 4½ years of filing date

Because of the complex nature of the above, professional advice is strongly recommended.

Obtaining UK trade mark registration

A trade mark is a word, device etc, which is used to identify a trader's goods and to distinguish such goods from others. If the trade mark is sufficiently distinctive, statutory·rights in it may be obtained through registration.

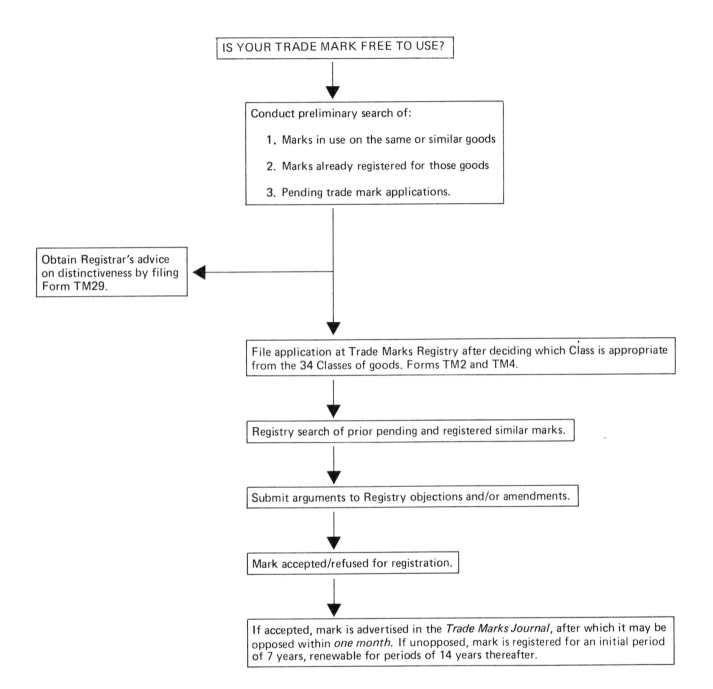

```
                    ┌─────────────────────────────────────┐
                    │ IS YOUR TRADE MARK FREE TO USE?      │
                    └─────────────────────────────────────┘
                                      │
                                      ▼
                    ┌─────────────────────────────────────┐
                    │ Conduct preliminary search of:       │
                    │                                      │
                    │   1. Marks in use on the same or     │
                    │      similar goods                   │
                    │   2. Marks already registered for    │
                    │      those goods                     │
                    │   3. Pending trade mark applications.│
                    └─────────────────────────────────────┘
```

Obtain Registrar's advice on distinctiveness by filing Form TM29.

File application at Trade Marks Registry after deciding which Class is appropriate from the 34 Classes of goods. Forms TM2 and TM4.

Registry search of prior pending and registered similar marks.

Submit arguments to Registry objections and/or amendments.

Mark accepted/refused for registration.

If accepted, mark is advertised in the *Trade Marks Journal*, after which it may be opposed within *one month*. If unopposed, mark is registered for an initial period of 7 years, renewable for periods of 14 years thereafter.

Professional advice is strongly recommended in all matters relating to trade marks in view of the possibility of confusion and/or passing off occurring, with resultant litigation.

Chapter 8

Beginning to Manage

Documentation for start-up

Paperwork should be kept to a minimum. Nevertheless, paper records are required to protect you and your business. Most of these items will be required before start-up:

	Dates		
	Designed	Ordered	Delivered
Letterhead			
Business card			
Publicity material			
Price-lists			
Order pad			
Invoice/delivery/credit note set			
Monthly statement			
Petty cash voucher book			
Cheque book			
Bank paying-in book			

The letterhead and business card may well be the first contact a customer has with your business.

Will they say about you what you want them to say?

In the case of a limited company, the letterhead must show the address of the registered office, the registration number, and Limited or Ltd, all or none of the directors, VAT number if registered.

Basic business records

No business can be properly run without adequate records. This short list covers the *absolute minimum* of information. Records should be written up daily or weekly, and be completely backed up by receipts, vouchers etc.

1. *Cash book*
   (a) Record cash sales and payments made from cash transactions.
   (b) Record payments in and out of bank.
   (c) Show VAT on payments as applicable.

2. *VAT records* (if applicable)
   (a) Show how VAT return figures have been calculated.
   (b) In addition, non-retailers must maintain a list of sales invoices issued.

3. *Petty cash book* (where applicable)
   Small cash expenses should be kept on an imprest basis and should show VAT where applicable.

4. *Wages book, wage slips*
   Summary information to meet the needs of the employee and the Inland Revenue.

5. *Order and delivery books*
   Purchases and sales, orders and deliveries.

6. *Overdue accounts book*
   Debtors and age analysis of debts for all credit sales.

Professional advice *from your accountant* should establish the most appropriate records for the business. If you follow his advice, it will also tend to reduce his fees.

Some businesses may find the services provided by a contract book-keeping service cost-effective.

The bank account

Few businesses can operate outside the banking system. These details should be covered well before start-up date.

1. *How many accounts?*

	Needed	Date arranged	Note
Business current account			Overdraft facility
Business deposit account			Interest rate?
Business loan accounts			
Personal current account			
Personal deposit account			
Personal loan account			
Personal 'tax' account			To cover future tax demands

Don't have more accounts than you need and can manage.

2. *Bank statements*

   Frequency (delete as applicable)
   Daily
   Weekly
   Monthly, or
   Quarterly

   The bank reconciliation (see below) should be made for each statement.

3. *Signatories*
   Obtain bank mandate form.
   Use crossed cheques.
   Name two signatories whenever practicable.

NB. Two signatories may lead the Inland Revenue to argue that a 'sole trader' is now a 'partnership'.
   Complete cheque book stubs fully and accurately.

4. *Charges*
   It all costs money. Discuss with your bank manager what you can sensibly do to minimise bank charges. Get quotations from other banks.

Bank reconciliations

A bank statement is produced by the bank at your request. A weekly statement would be right for many businesses.

A bank position or report shows your own latest figures of your bank account.

The *bank statement* and the *bank position or report* should be reconciled from time to time – often weekly. This format shows how to do the reconciliation.

1. Balance according to bank statement £

2. Add monies paid in but not cleared by the bank (deduct if bank statement shows an overdraft) £

3. Deduct cheques drawn but not entered by the bank (add if bank statment shows an overdraft) £ _____

4. Balance according to books £ _____

   Difference, if any £ _____

Any difference should be investigated immediately.

NB. Interest on any overdraft, and bank charges, will be debited to the account automatically and usually every quarter.

Purchasing practice

Good purchasing is a vital element in all businesses but especially in retailing and manufacturing. This checklist has been designed as a guide to purchasing.

Action	*Check*
1. Analyse goods to be purchased	Specification complete, up to date and accurate
2. Identify vendors who can supply	Provision for quality assurance Competitiveness Financial status
3. Issue enquiries	Instructions clear Terms of purchase specified Delivery requirements Any additional requirements
4. Receipt of quotations	Equipment described meets specification Analyse vendor's 'Conditions of Sale' and compare with your 'Conditions of Purchase' Price variation or fixed price? Payment terms and quantity discounts/rebates Validity Warranty Delivery period
5. Evaluation of quotations	Comparisons 'like for like' Total cost of order in consideration of any advance payments Current workload/financial status Delivery period
6. Choose best option	After considering 4. and 5. above
7. Place order	Terms of order are agreeable to vendor and purchaser Any additional requirements
8. Expedite acknowledgement	Check 'Terms of Acknowledgement' are in agreement with 'Terms of Order'
9. Monitor progress of order	Inspection/expeditor reports as necessary
10. Approve invoice payment	Check goods received in good order Verify any extras/reductions Obtain Certificates of Ownership if appropriate.

The routine of business accounting

There is no substitute for keeping up to date in financial control. Check that you meet these suggestions:

	Daily	Weekly	Monthly	Quarterly	Six-monthly
Check cash takings against till roll (Retail)	✓				
Note cash position	✓				
Write up day books	✓				
Raise invoices	✓				
Bank cash/cheques	✓				
Check deliveries against delivery notes	✓				
Pay wages		✓			
Draw cheques		✓			
Prepare weekly summaries		✓			
Do bank reconciliation		✓	or ✓		
Follow up overdues		✓	✓		
Issue statements			✓		
Total and summarise ledgers			✓		
Authorise salaries, tax and NI			✓		
Compare actual with budgeted sales and expenses			✓		
Update cash flow projections			✓	or ✓	
Take raw material, work in progress and finished goods stocks			✓	or ✓	
Prepare age analysis of debtors and creditors		✓	or ✓		
Pay VAT				✓	
Prepare trading account			✓	or ✓	or ✓
Prepare interim accounts			✓	or ✓	or ✓
Complete tax planning				✓	or ✓
Do sales and expenses budget updates				✓	

Precisely who is responsible for each item of work?

How do you know it is being done properly and on time?

Annual accounts

Annual accounts should be completed within a few weeks of the financial year end, and include:

1. Profit and loss account
2. Balance sheet
3. Sources and application of funds (companies)
4. Notes and analyses
5. Directors' Report (companies)

Annual accounts are a legal requirement for companies. Sole traders and partnerships need them for the taxman, and probably the bank. Usually they are prepared by your accountant.

Annual accounts provide insufficient information for the running of most businesses. To keep control of a business you must have constant up-to-date information, which should be discussed with your accountant.

	Tick your plan		
	Monthly	**Quarterly**	**Six-monthly**
How often do you want to have:			
Trading accounts	☐	☐	☐
Profit and loss accounts	☐	☐	☐
Balance sheets	☐	☐	☐
Sources and application of funds statements	☐	☐	☐
Working capital movements	☐	☐	☐
Summarised cash movements	☐	☐	☐
Cash flow projections	☐	☐	☐
Discussion of current trends and prospects	☐	☐	☐
Review of overall plans	☐	☐	☐

NB. Some of the above are alternatives depending on the amount of information considered necessary for effective control.

Marginal product costing

As a prelude to any sales, the businessman should calculate his cost build-up using a format similar to this.

Direct material costs

	Cost	x	Usage*	=	Materials cost
Materials	£ per unit	x	Units per product, job etc	=	£ per product, job etc
(i)					
(ii)					
(iii)					
(iv)					
(v)					
(vi)					
(vii)					
	Total Direct materials cost (A)			=	£

* Including wastage/losses

Direct labour costs

	Cost**	x	Usage	=	Labour cost
Operations	£ per unit	x	Standard hours per product, job etc	=	£ per product, job etc
(i)					
(ii)					
(iii)					
(iv)					
	Total Direct labour cost (B)			=	£

** Full cost, not wage rate

Total variable cost   C = (A) + (B) =   £ _____

Overhead costs   *Annual Cost £*

For example:
Marketing costs
Travel
Rent, rates
Insurance
Post, telephone
Heating, lighting
Repairs, maintenance
Administration salaries, NI
Professional fees
Loan and overdraft interest
Depreciation
Others

Total cost   (D)

Products

1   2   3 etc

Selling price (£)   (E)

Product, jobs etc (number)   (F)

Total sales (£)   (G = E x F)

Total direct materials (£)   (H = A x F)

Total direct labour (£)   (I = B x F)

Total variable cost (£)   (J = H + I)

Contribution to overheads
and profit (£)   (K = G − J)

Overhead   (D)
cost (£)

Profit (£)   (K − D)

Gross margin   =   Contribution x 100 $(\frac{K}{G} \times 100)$
%   £ Sales

These figures may help with:
- New price structures
- Changes to product mix
- Adjustments to size of labour force
- Make or buy-in decisions
- Capital expenditure to save labour costs

Margins and mark-ups

Business people involved with retailers need to be familiar with these two expressions.

Margin   = $\dfrac{\text{Selling price} - \text{buying price}}{\text{Selling price}}$ x   100 =   %

Mark-up   = $\dfrac{\text{Selling price} - \text{buying price}}{\text{Buying price}}$ x   100 =   %

Try these calculations :

Selling price (excl VAT)	Buying price (excl VAT)	Percentage margin	Percentage mark-up
£1.00	50p		
£1.50	£1.00		
£2.66	£2.00		
£3.00	£2.40		
£4.00	£3.60		

97

Cash collection

A sale is not a sale until it is paid for!

Wherever credit is given, cash flow can *always* be improved — by improved cash collection.

Improve cash collection by

1. Having a named person responsible for cash collection.

2. Setting cash collection targets and measuring performance.

3. Taking out credit references and setting credit limits.

4. Specifying payment date on:
   - quotation/estimate
   - price-list
   - delivery note (file signed copy)
   - invoice statment

   And mentioning it in all relevant conversations.

5. Issuing invoice immediately and accurately on completion/delivery of work. Cross reference to order numbers. Deliver to correct address as specified by the buyer.

6. Establishing date of automatic follow-up by:
   - statement
   - letter of demand
   - telephone   } Don't be taken in by excuses!
   - stop supply
   - letter of legal action

7. Considering prompt payment discounts, deposits, prepayments and stage payments.

8. Proceedings through:
   County Court (Limit £5,000)
   Small claims procedure (Limit £500)
   High Court.

9. Pressing for execution of any court order.

10. Ceasing to supply slow payers on credit : use proforma invoice.

11. Considering non-recourse factoring and bad debt insurance.

Is credit given measured?

Days

1. $\dfrac{\text{Total outstandings} \times 365}{\text{Annual sales}} =$ ☐

   or

2. Total outstandings offset against immediate past invoices = ☐

3. What were comparable figures:

   last year? ☐

   in previous year? ☐

4. What do competitors give? ☐

The integrated computer accounting package

To the question 'Should I buy an integrated computer accounting system?' there is no immediate answer.

Take expert advice, and remember that *rarely will the computer bring cost reductions*, but it may enable more work to be handled.

Interrelations in the integrated package

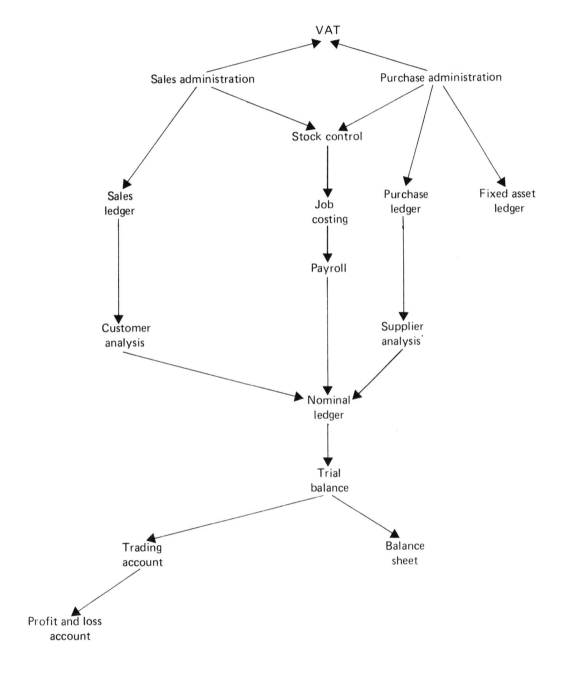

99

Credit cards

From the point of view of a merchant or trader, the use of a credit card can be a considerable advantage. Following on the well-known Visa and Access cards, progressive towns such as Wilmslow in Cheshire have now introduced their own charge card.

Advantages of the credit card

1. The merchant obtains immediate credit on depositing the sales voucher with the appropriate bank or finance house.

2. The funds are normally credited without recourse, thereby eliminating a guarantee of payment by telephone.

3. As an easy and trouble-free method of payment, it can attract a custom which might not otherwise have been forthcoming.

4. Mail and telephone order facilities may be available to the merchant. Retailers' own cards are also available.

5. The bulk of the administration is done centrally, and there is little or no necessity for extra resources to maintain accounts.

6. Normally only one VAT invoice is required each month for the commission.

7. Sales vouchers of £10 and under are normally accepted as VAT invoices, and this ensures that paperwork in relation to VAT is then kept to an absolute minimum.

8. Company credit cards are now available for directors and employees to meet their expenses for payment by direct debit. This scheme features personalised cards for the authorised company employee, produces a company statement, and narrative memoranda for each company employee. These are sent to the company monthly and give the company an average of 17 days' credit.

Costs of the credit card

1. There is normally a joining fee, paid only once. For example, the VAT inclusive charge for a credit card varies from £20 to £100.

2. There is a service charge on each transaction, which is normally between 3 and 5 per cent.

3. Be sure that the cost of accepting credit card transactions does not unacceptably reduce your mark-up (for example, on a single low-cost item with an already slender margin).

4. For company credit cards there are various conditions, including an overall credit limit. Costs range from either £3 per annum per card, and 20p per debit entry, to £12 per annum per card, with no entry charge.

Obtaining a credit card facility

1. Application to the issuing bank or finance house.

2. Visit by credit card consultant.

3. Completion of essential details on application form.

4. Acceptance.

Which of these British Telecom services will you use?

Facility	Apply	Service	Notes	Information required ✓
Bureaufax	Area Sales Office or dial 100 and ask for freefone Bureaufax	Facsimile service in the UK and abroad	To send or receive facsimile copies of documents	
Business communications service	Area Sales Office or dial 01-936 2242	Design, specify, install and support complex international communications	Companies operating in the international environment	
Confravision	Area Sales Office	Conference service between distant points		
Customer controlled forwarding	Area Sales Office	Diverts incoming calls to other offices or locations	Programmable up to ten numbers	
Europages	Area Sales Office	Directory covering 130,000 European companies	Produced by British Telecom Yellow Pages	
Freefone	Dial 100 and ask for freefone 8948	Client can now sell their service, products or company image	No numbers to be remembered by a customer. Freefone name encourages people to get in touch	
International leased telegraph message switching service	Area Sales Office or dial 01-726 2064	Private international links	Links customer UK office(s) with offices or agents overseas	
International packet switching service	Area Sales Office or dial 01-936 2750	Data communications service	Wide variety of communication needs and applications. Linked to numerous international computer networks	
Kilo stream	Area Sales Office	Private circuit service	Offers high speed data links	
Phone-ins	Area Sales Office or dial 01-357 3862	Rental equipment on which you can broadcast a recorded message		
Packet switch stream	Area Sales Office	Public data service	Widely used for computer communication	
Prestel	Area Sales Office or dial 100 and ask for freefone Prestel Sales	Public viewdata service	Links adapted television screens to computers through ordinary telephone lines	
Sat Stream	Dial 01-936 2350	Private high speed communications	Transmission through small-dish satellite earth terminals	
Telecom Gold	Area Sales Office or dial 01-403 6777	24-hour public electronic mail service		
Telecom Silver	Dial 01-379 0663	Checkcard service	Combines a modern telephone-check phone and a talking computer to provide protection against the fraudulent use of credit cards	
Phone power	Area Sales Office or dial 100 and ask for freefone Phone Power	Telephone consultancy service	New service to show how the telephone expertly used can improve a business's performance	
Telex equipment	Area Sales Office	Hard copy print out of communications keyboarded by sender	Ask for 'Business Sales' for your locality	
Call connect systems	Area Sales Office		As above	
External lines Business Residential	Area Sales Office	Products & Services: for the business for the home	As above Ask for 'Sales' for your locality	

Mail services

Can your business survive with the Royal Mail? In addition to the basic delivery service, the Post Office provide a range of additional services. Which of the following will help your business? Current prices are available in the 'Postal Rates' booklet.

Facility	Apply	Service	Notes	Investigation needed ✓
Postcode	Post Office	–	Required for business stationery	
PO Box number	Post Master	Collect or deliver parcels	Provides earlier availability of correspondence	
Business reply	Form P36	1st or 2nd class mail	Application needs sample envelope	
Freepost	Form P2797	2nd class mail	Usually for direct response sales campaigns	
Recorded delivery	Post Office	Signed delivery	Provides proof of delivery	
Registered post	Post Office	Insured, signed delivery	Mainly for valuables	
Franking machines	Three manufacturers	Mail out franking	Involves a rental charge. Gives advertising and security benefits	
Datapost	Post Office	Next day delivery	Cash or credit. Also international	
Express post	Post Office	Same day delivery	Local and intercity tariffs	
COD	Post Office	Cash on delivery	Collection for items of 22.5 kg and over	
Leaflet distribution	Post Office	Door to door	May be directed to Acorn Classification of Residential Neighbourhood targets	
Parcels	Post Office	Three-day service	Also local routes, max 25 kg	
Direct mail	Post Office	Same day posting	1000 free trial scheme	

Chapter 9

Employment

Taking on an employee

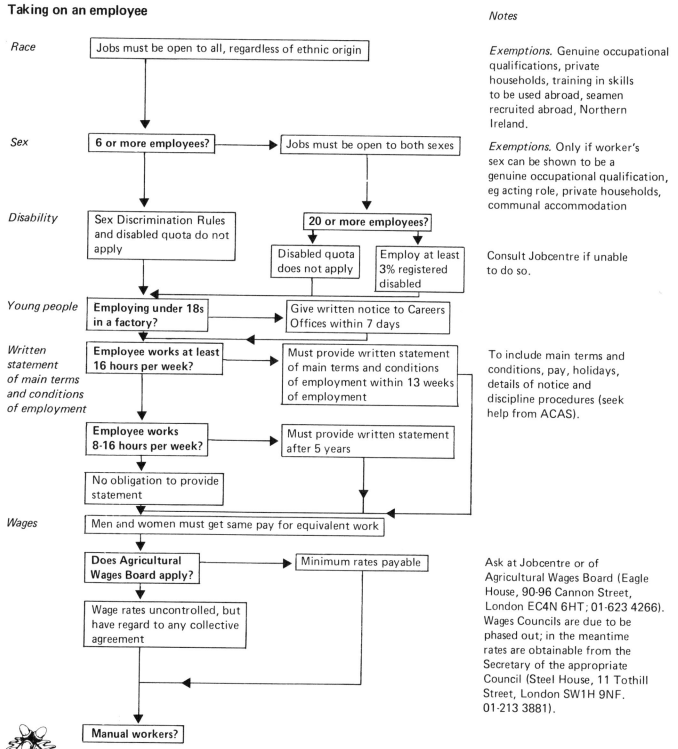

Race — Jobs must be open to all, regardless of ethnic origin

Notes

Exemptions. Genuine occupational qualifications, private households, training in skills to be used abroad, seamen recruited abroad, Northern Ireland.

Sex — 6 or more employees? → Jobs must be open to both sexes

Exemptions. Only if worker's sex can be shown to be a genuine occupational qualification, eg acting role, private households, communal accommodation

Disability — Sex Discrimination Rules and disabled quota do not apply

20 or more employees?

Disabled quota does not apply

Employ at least 3% registered disabled

Consult Jobcentre if unable to do so.

Young people — Employing under 18s in a factory? → Give written notice to Careers Offices within 7 days

Written statement of main terms and conditions of employment — Employee works at least 16 hours per week? → Must provide written statement of main terms and conditions of employment within 13 weeks of employment

To include main terms and conditions, pay, holidays, details of notice and discipline procedures (seek help from ACAS).

Employee works 8-16 hours per week? → Must provide written statement after 5 years

No obligation to provide statement

Wages — Men and women must get same pay for equivalent work

Does Agricultural Wages Board apply? → Minimum rates payable

Wage rates uncontrolled, but have regard to any collective agreement

Ask at Jobcentre or of Agricultural Wages Board (Eagle House, 90-96 Cannon Street, London EC4N 6HT; 01-623 4266). Wages Councils are due to be phased out; in the meantime rates are obtainable from the Secretary of the appropriate Council (Steel House, 11 Tothill Street, London SW1H 9NF. 01-213 3881).

Manual workers?

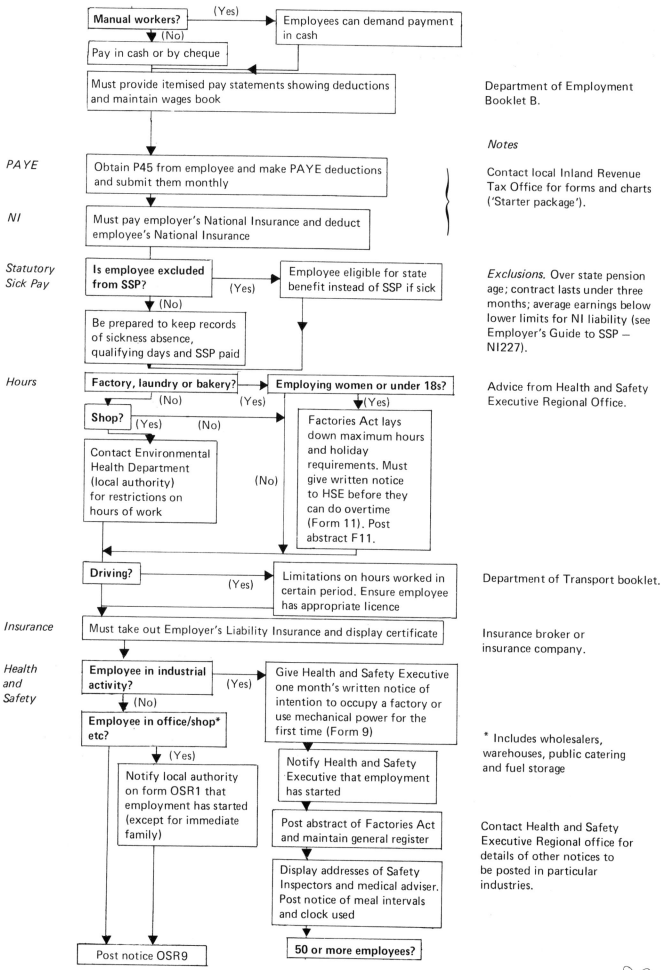

Manual workers? — (Yes) → Employees can demand payment in cash

(No) → Pay in cash or by cheque

Must provide itemised pay statements showing deductions and maintain wages book

Department of Employment Booklet B.

Notes

PAYE — Obtain P45 from employee and make PAYE deductions and submit them monthly

NI — Must pay employer's National Insurance and deduct employee's National Insurance

Contact local Inland Revenue Tax Office for forms and charts ('Starter package').

Statutory Sick Pay — **Is employee excluded from SSP?** — (Yes) → Employee eligible for state benefit instead of SSP if sick

(No) → Be prepared to keep records of sickness absence, qualifying days and SSP paid

Exclusions. Over state pension age; contract lasts under three months; average earnings below lower limits for NI liability (see Employer's Guide to SSP — NI227).

Hours — **Factory, laundry or bakery?** — (No) → **Employing women or under 18s?** — (Yes) →

(Yes) → **Shop?** — (Yes) → Contact Environmental Health Department (local authority) for restrictions on hours of work

(No) →

Employing women or under 18s? (Yes) → Factories Act lays down maximum hours and holiday requirements. Must give written notice to HSE before they can do overtime (Form 11). Post abstract F11.

(No) →

Advice from Health and Safety Executive Regional Office.

Driving? — (Yes) → Limitations on hours worked in certain period. Ensure employee has appropriate licence

Department of Transport booklet.

Insurance — Must take out Employer's Liability Insurance and display certificate

Insurance broker or insurance company.

Health and Safety — **Employee in industrial activity?** — (Yes) → Give Health and Safety Executive one month's written notice of intention to occupy a factory or use mechanical power for the first time (Form 9)

(No) → **Employee in office/shop* etc?** — (Yes) → Notify local authority on form OSR1 that employment has started (except for immediate family)

Notify Health and Safety Executive that employment has started

Post abstract of Factories Act and maintain general register

Display addresses of Safety Inspectors and medical adviser. Post notice of meal intervals and clock used

* Includes wholesalers, warehouses, public catering and fuel storage

Contact Health and Safety Executive Regional office for details of other notices to be posted in particular industries.

Post notice OSR9

50 or more employees?

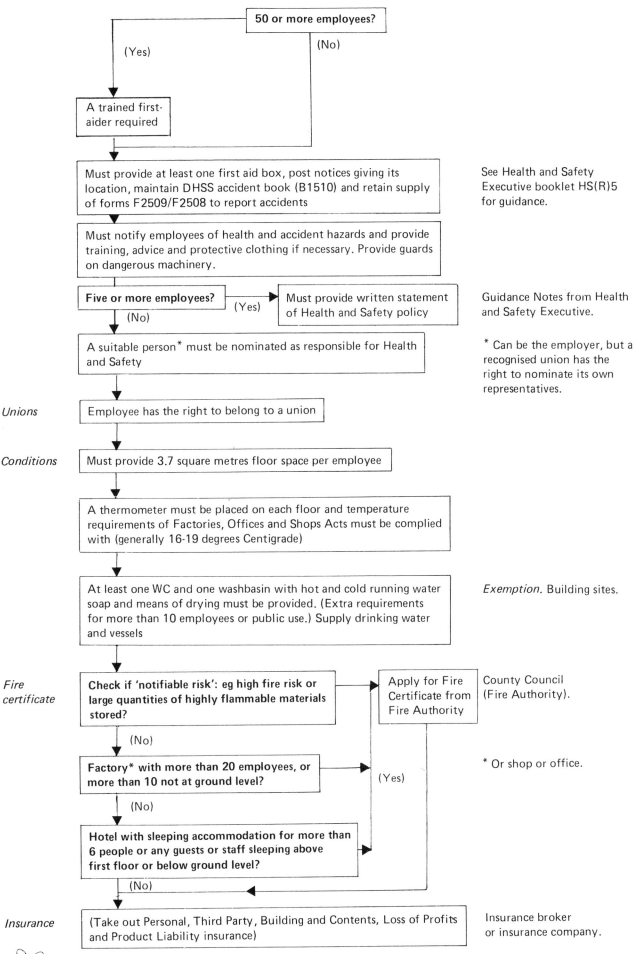

50 or more employees?

(Yes)   (No)

A trained first-aider required

Must provide at least one first aid box, post notices giving its location, maintain DHSS accident book (B1510) and retain supply of forms F2509/F2508 to report accidents

See Health and Safety Executive booklet HS(R)5 for guidance.

Must notify employees of health and accident hazards and provide training, advice and protective clothing if necessary. Provide guards on dangerous machinery.

Five or more employees?
(No)   (Yes)

Must provide written statement of Health and Safety policy

Guidance Notes from Health and Safety Executive.

A suitable person* must be nominated as responsible for Health and Safety

* Can be the employer, but a recognised union has the right to nominate its own representatives.

Unions   Employee has the right to belong to a union

Conditions   Must provide 3.7 square metres floor space per employee

A thermometer must be placed on each floor and temperature requirements of Factories, Offices and Shops Acts must be complied with (generally 16-19 degrees Centigrade)

At least one WC and one washbasin with hot and cold running water soap and means of drying must be provided. (Extra requirements for more than 10 employees or public use.) Supply drinking water and vessels

Exemption. Building sites.

Fire certificate

Check if 'notifiable risk': eg high fire risk or large quantities of highly flammable materials stored?

Apply for Fire Certificate from Fire Authority

County Council (Fire Authority).

(No)

Factory* with more than 20 employees, or more than 10 not at ground level?

(Yes)

* Or shop or office.

(No)

Hotel with sleeping accommodation for more than 6 people or any guests or staff sleeping above first floor or below ground level?

(No)

Insurance   (Take out Personal, Third Party, Building and Contents, Loss of Profits and Product Liability insurance)

Insurance broker or insurance company.

Sources of employees

As an aid to finding the appropriately qualified person for employment, this list has been prepared:

- Existing employees
- Other businesses
- Relatives and friends
- Jobcentre
- Careers Office
- Placement Officers at schools colleges and polytechnics
- Youth Training Scheme ⎫
- Training Workshop ⎭ Managing agents, Jobcentre, or Careers Office
- Job advertisements — local press, radio/TV
- Professional and Executive Register
- Recruitment and placement agencies
- Personnel managers handling a redundancy programme

Planning the employment interview

In view of the high costs to the business of poor recruitment, this list is a summary of the minimum essential preparation.

Is there a *written*: Job Description?

Personal Profile?

What *must* you learn from the interview?

....

....

List the following:

Rates of pay
— immediate
— after training
— overtime
— bonuses, commissions
Hours of work/working week
— breaks
Holidays
Other benefits
— vehicle
— health insurance
— pension

Have you checked:

- — How income tax will be deducted?
- — National Insurance?
- — Statutory Sick Pay?
- — Equal Opportunities and similar legislation?

Can the workplace be visited?

Who will make up the interviewing team?

....

....

....

Personal profile

The employment of the right person in a small business is vital. This presentation will cover employees, partners, working directors, and even, to an extent, new shareholders.

Qualifications for employment	
Required (= must have)	*Desirable (= nice to have)*

1. Age

2. Education

3. Training

4. Experience

5. Abilities/skills

6. Ambitions/future

7. Attitudes

8. Marital status

9. Health

10. Location

This profile will help a business to remain within Equal Opportunities and Sex Discrimination legislation.

Does your application form help you to get this information?

Employees' statutory rights

For employees working more than 16 hours per week, and subject to various lengths of service, there are statutory rights in respect of:

1. Written particulars of the terms of employment

2. Wage or salary pay statement

3. Notice of termination of employment

4. Time off for public duties

5. Provisions in connection with pregnancy, maternity and the right to return to work

6. Guaranteed payments

7. Payment when suspended on medical grounds

8. Redundancy

9. Dismissal

10. Statutory Sick Pay (SSP)

11. Health and safety at work

The business should have a legal adviser capable of providing guidance to ensure proper respect for employment law. The solicitor would also act for the business when an employee or former employee made claims arising from termination of employment or disciplinary action.

NB. Businesses employing *fewer than 20 persons* do have some dispensations under employment protection legislation:

- No requirement to employ disabled persons
- No requirement to meet equal pay obligations
- Two years' continuous service by employee before a claim for unfair dismissal can be made.

Additional reference

Employment Protection (Consolidation) Act 1978.

Pay As You Earn (PAYE) and National Insurance (NI)

Immediately in the case of a limited company, and very early in the life of a sole trader, the business must act as a tax gatherer for the government. This flow chart shows the weekly, monthly and annual routines to be observed.

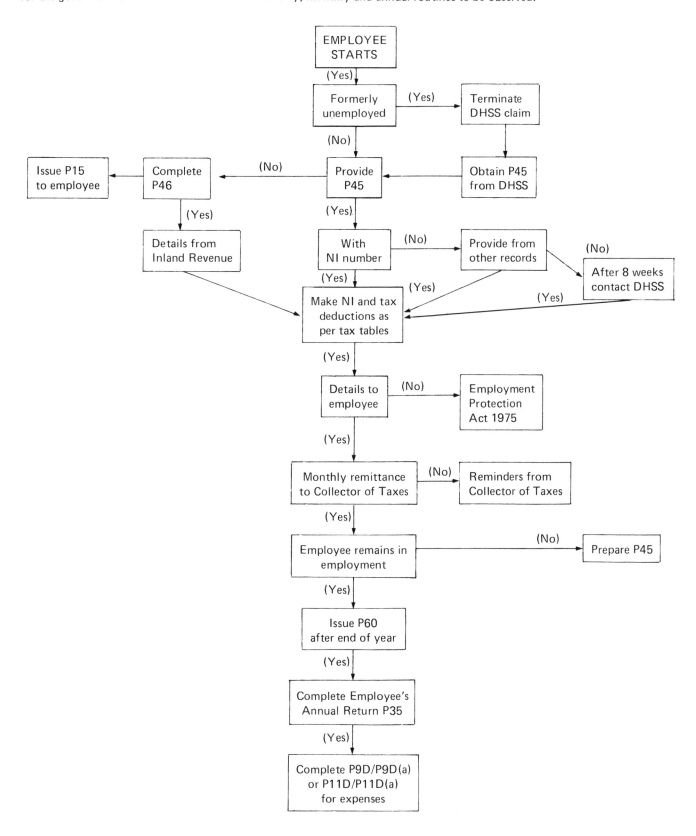

Further help may be drawn from the Tax Office, DHSS, your accountant or commercial payroll services.

National Insurance payments

All four classes of National Insurance contributions could affect the smaller business. These flowcharts show how payments should be handled.

Class 1 contributions for employed persons

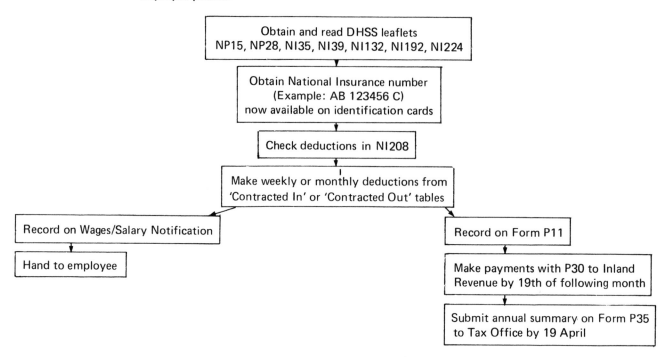

NB. Directors are also employees. Reduced contributions are payable by those who hold a Certificate of Election or a Certificate of Reduced Liability.

Class 2 contributions for self-employed persons

NB. Self-employed persons are *not* eligible for Unemployment Benefit, Industrial Injuries Benefit or earnings related benefits.

Class 3 contributions

Class 3 contributions are voluntary, and may be made by persons not gainfully employed in Great Britain. The fixed contribution may be paid by:

● Direct debit
● Stamping a card
● Lump sum payment at end of tax year.

Class 4 contributions for self-employed persons

Class 4 contributions are akin to an additional income tax. The contributions are collected by the Inland Revenue alongside Schedule D liabilities and relate to taxable profits between upper and lower limits.

Statutory Sick Pay (SSP)

The SSP Scheme has been in force since 6 April 1983. For those not familiar with its operation, their solicitor or accountant will provide help. These notes provide a brief introduction to the subject. Please see also leaflet NI 227.

Employee	**Employer**	*Notes*
	ESTABLISH NOTIFICATION RULES AND QUALIFYING DATES	
Goes sick		
Phones to —	NOMINATED PERSON	Appointed to note absence
	Logs in	
	ABSENCE RECORD	Official record of absence, can be inspected by DHSS. Contains other basic details of QUALIFYING DAYS PAYMENTS — to be kept for three years
Returns to work Completes ABSENCE STATEMENT Provides DOCTOR'S NOTE for absences above 7 days	Retains document(s)	
	Makes SSP payments	Record on Form P11
	Deducts SSP payments made from settlement with Inland Revenue	
	Annual summary	Use Form P14

111

Subcontractors' tax certificates

For some industries, notably the construction industry, there are benefits to both the contractor and the subcontractor if the latter holds a 714 certificate (Department of Employment)

1. *Start-up as an uncertified subcontractor.*

   Contractor deducts tax at 30 per cent, Form SC60.
   Contractor pays deductions to Inland Revenue.
   Subcontractor registers as self-employed with local tax office.
   Inland Revenue makes adjustments after end of tax year.
   Subcontractor pays own Class 2 National Insurance contribution.
   Subcontractor signs off DHSS benefits.

2. *Subcontractor applies for 714 certificate:* the authorities are unlikely to issue a 714 until some significant time after the start-up.

   Subcontractor must be UK based in relevant industry.
   Subcontractor must have good record of employment.
   Subcontractor must have good record of tax and NI contribution payments.
   Subcontractor must have proper business records and facilities.

3. *Certified subcontractor advises contractor.*

   Relieves contractor of administration.
   Subcontractor issues 715 voucher for every payment.
   Subcontractor maintains necessary records.
   Subcontractor makes returns to Inspector of Taxes.

NB. The 714 Certificate exists in four forms:

For individuals	714I
For partnerships	714P
For certain companies	714C
For special situations	714S

The *contractor* has an obligation to check:

- Names and photographs on 714I, 714P, 714S
- Expiry date
- Identify of bearer

to avoid tax liability.

Health and safety at work: Checklist

Under the Health and Safety at Work Act 1974, the employer (even if he is self-employed) has major responsibilities which may be tested through these questions. Both your solicitor and the Health and Safety Executive can help with uncertainties.

The location

Access	Is it adequate?
Neighbours	Will they harm your staff (dust, smell, noise etc)?
	Will you harm their staff (dust, smell, noise etc)?

The premises

Space	Is it big enough?
Ventilation	Is it adequate?
Heating	Is it adequate?
Lighting	Is it adequate?
Electrical installation	Is it in good condition?
Fire precautions	Are escapes marked and assembly areas identified?
	Are fire extinguishers of correct type?
	Is a fire alarm fitted and tested?
Floors, stairs	Are they sound and non-slip?
Toilets	Are they in a satisfactory condition?
	Are there enough?
Safety audit	When was it last done?

Equipment

First aid	Have you got a first aid kit? Safety showers? Protective gear?
Machinery	Is it properly installed?
	Is it properly guarded?
Statutory inspections	Has a surveyor from your insurers examined your:
	— air receiver or compressor
	— steam boiler
	— lifting tackle
	— cranes
	— lifts
	— pressure vessels?

Materials handled

Toxic	Are precautions adequate?
	Effluents and waste disposal?
Inflammable*	Are precautions adequate?
	Flameproof equipment?
Corrosive	Are precautions adequate?
Dust/fume control	Is local exhaust ventilation required?
Protective clothing	Is any required? Is it issued and used?

* Flammable has the same meaning, ie easily set on fire.

Environment

Noise	Is your process very noisy?
	What precautions do you need to take?

Systems of work

Methods of work	Are they carefully thought out?
	Are they safe?
Training	Do your employees know what to do?
	Have they been warned about potential risks and the precautions to be taken?
	What is the existing pattern of evacuation drills?
Supervision	How do you make sure they work in accordance with instructions?

Others

Safety	If you have more than five employees, then you must have a written safety policy.
Safety representatives	If you have a recognised trade union, they may appoint safety representatives.
Notification of accidents	If a serious accident happens in your premises, you must inform the relevant authority as soon as possible.
Forms	If your premises are subject to the Factories Act 1961 or Offices, Shops and Railway Premises Act 1963, then you must display an abstract of the relevant Act at your premises.
	If you intend to open a factory you must notify the Health and Safety Executive of your intention not less than 28 days before you open it.

Are Big Problems on the Way?

Overtrading, a problem associated with success

Some problems arise from *success*. Difficulties may be caused by expanding the business more quickly than cash resources can stand. This is *overtrading*.

This checklist may help you decide whether overtrading is a threat to your business.

Tick those which apply to your business

Customers clamouring for goods ☐

Stocks increasing ☐

Debtors increasing ☐

Creditors crying out for payment ☐

Suppliers threatening to cut off supplies ☐

Overdraft limit breached : bank refusing to lend more ☐

For remedies, see page 115.

The cash flow problem

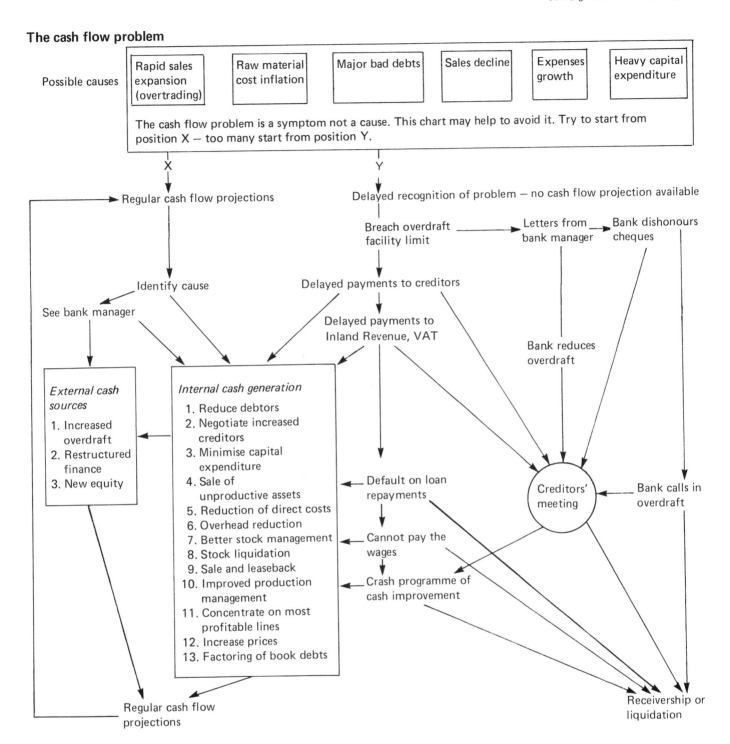

Possible causes

| Rapid sales expansion (overtrading) | Raw material cost inflation | Major bad debts | Sales decline | Expenses growth | Heavy capital expenditure |

The cash flow problem is a symptom not a cause. This chart may help to avoid it. Try to start from position X — too many start from position Y.

X

Y

Regular cash flow projections

Delayed recognition of problem — no cash flow projection available

Breach overdraft facility limit → Letters from bank manager → Bank dishonours cheques

Identify cause

Delayed payments to creditors

See bank manager

Delayed payments to Inland Revenue, VAT

Bank reduces overdraft

External cash sources

1. Increased overdraft
2. Restructured finance
3. New equity

Internal cash generation

1. Reduce debtors
2. Negotiate increased creditors
3. Minimise capital expenditure
4. Sale of unproductive assets
5. Reduction of direct costs
6. Overhead reduction
7. Better stock management
8. Stock liquidation
9. Sale and leaseback
10. Improved production management
11. Concentrate on most profitable lines
12. Increase prices
13. Factoring of book debts

Default on loan repayments

Cannot pay the wages

Crash programme of cash improvement

Creditors' meeting

Bank calls in overdraft

Regular cash flow projections

Receivership or liquidation

Take to the bank proof of what you have already done to improve the situation

Growth, survival or extinction?

Knowing where the business is has consistently proved to be a key to survival in difficult markets and growth in buoyant ones. Pages 116-21 give simple formats for control information in typical smaller businesses. The items are set out in this order:

Responsibilities of the management

Sales and marketing effectiveness

Orders and shipments

Employment status

Cash

    Liquidity

    Debtors

    Creditors

Profitability

    Profit and loss account

    Break-even

Assets

    Balance sheet

    Control ratios

Business planning

    Cash flow projections

    Financial planning

    Management action plan

Responsibilities of the management

Who is responsible for:	To whom responsible?	Date of last report
Cash management		
Cash collection		
Costing		
Management information		
Accounts and book-keeping		
Invoicing		
Sales		
Marketing		
Pricing		
Customer complaints		
Employee relations		
Recruitment		
Security		
Production		
— costs		
— quality		
— rate		
Purchasing		
Other key elements in the business		

Sales and marketing effectiveness

	Last month		Prior month		Year to date	
	Number	*Value of (monthly) business*	*Number*	*Value of (monthly) business*	*Number*	*Value of (monthly) business*
New accounts won						
Existing accounts lost						
Enquiries obtained						
Quotations put out						
Firm orders gained						
Firm orders as repeat business						
Tenders notified						
Tenders submitted						
Tenders awarded						
Market trends reported in national / regional / local } statistics						

Orders and shipments

Firm and despatchable orders on hand:

Volume   units

Value   £

		Orders completed			Orders booked for completion			
		3 months ago	*2 months ago*	*Last month*	*This month*	*Forward months*		
						2	3	4
High contribution products	£							
Medium contribution products	£							
Low contribution products	£							
Total sales	£							
Gross margin	£							
Overheads	£							
Gross Margin — Overheads	£							
Factory or business loading	%							
Orders *not* despatched								
— supplier fault	£							
— our fault	£							

117

Employment status

	Last month	Prior month
Desired number of employees		
Full time		
Part time	———	———
TOTAL Full-time equivalents	———	———
Employed at month end		
Vacancies unfilled		

	Year to date
Employees departed in month	
Resigned	
Dismissed	
Redundant	
Retired	
New employees recruited	
Absenteeism rate	

Cash

LIQUIDITY	Now	Last week	Prior week	Last month
Cash in hand				
Balance per bank statement				
Payments drawn, not presented to bank				
Collections not credited to bank account				
Adjusted bank position				
Overdraft limit agreed with bank				

DEBTORS		Last month	Prior month	Previous month
Total debtors	(a)			
Moving annual sales + VAT	(b)			
$\dfrac{\text{Debtors}}{\text{Sales}} = \dfrac{(a)}{(b)} \times 100$		%	%	%

In seasonal businesses, these percentages should be compared with figures from the corresponding period in past years.

CREDITORS		Last month	Prior month	Previous month
Trade creditors	(c)			
Moving annual trade purchases	(d)			
$\dfrac{\text{Creditors}}{\text{Purchases}} = \dfrac{(c)}{(d)} \times 100$		%	%	%

In seasonal businesses, these percentages should be compared with figures from the corresponding period in past years.

Profitability

PROFIT AND LOSS ACCOUNT

Current month				Financial Year to date			
Last year	This year			Last year	This year		
Actual	Actual	Budget		Actual	Actual	Budget	Variance
			Sales				
			Cost of sales				
			Gross margin (B)				
			Selling costs				
			Distribution costs				
			Administration costs				
			Occupational costs				
			Research and development costs				
			Total overhead costs (A)				
			Profit before interest and tax				
			Interest				
			Profit before tax				

BREAK-EVEN

	Total overheads (A)		
	Gross margin % (B)		
	Break-even sales:		
	$\dfrac{A}{B} \times 100$		

Assets

BALANCE SHEET

	Last financial year end	Last interim report	Current interim report
Fixed assets			
Land, buildings			
Fixtures, fittings and equipment			
Motor vehicles			
Total fixed assets			
Investments			
Current assets			
Stock			
Prepayments			
Debtors			
Bank			
Cash			
Total current assets			
Total assets			
Current liabilities			
Creditors — Trade			
— Others			
Accruals			
Overdraft			
Total current liabilities			
Long-term liabilities			
Proprietor's capital (net worth)			
Total liabilities and net worth			

CONTROL RATIOS

MAT is used below to stand for Moving Annual Total, ie, running 12-month figures.

	Last financial year end	Last interim report	Current interim report
Liquidity			
$\dfrac{\text{Current assets}}{\text{Current liabilities}}$			
$\dfrac{\text{Current assets} - \text{Stock}}{\text{Current liabilities}}$			
Working capital			
$\dfrac{\text{Stock}}{\text{MAT cost of sales}}$			
$\dfrac{\text{Debtors}}{\text{MAT sales}} \times 100\%$ (see page 118)			
$\dfrac{\text{Creditors}}{\text{MAT purchases}} \times 100\%$ (see page 118)			
Financial structure			
$\dfrac{\text{Total liabilities}}{\text{Net worth}}$			
$\dfrac{\text{MAT profit before interest and tax}}{\text{MAT interest paid}}$			
Profitability			
$\dfrac{\text{MAT profit before interest and tax}}{\text{Total assets}}$			
$\dfrac{\text{MAT pfofit before interest and tax}}{\text{MAT sales}}$			
$\dfrac{\text{MAT sales}}{\text{Total assets}}$			

Business planning

CASH FLOW PROJECTIONS

	This month	Month					
		2	3	4	5	6	etc
Opening balance (reconciled)							
Cash receipts							
Total inflow							
Cash payments							
Total outflow							
Closing balance							
Agreed bank overdraft facility							

FINANCIAL PLANNING
At the heart of business planning is forecast performance in these three areas:

	Current year by month	Next year by quarter	Following year
Cash flow (for format for first six months see above)	✓	✓	✓
Profit and loss account	✓	✓	✓
Balance sheet	✓	✓	✓

MANAGEMENT ACTION PLAN
Arising from the foregoing analyses, an action plan can be drawn up and assigned.

Major objectives*	To be done by	Completion date

* Clear and understandable
Challenging but attainable
Measurable
Relevant
Consistent with other objectives.

Heading for business ruin

Business failure runs at 80 per cent of all start-ups within their first five years. Studies like John Argenti's (in *Corporate Collapse — the causes and the symptoms*, McGraw-Hill, 1976) have shown identifying marks. *Score your enterprise* by marking NIL where you are uncertain whether the item is clearly visible in your business. Where the item is clearly visible, score the points indicated. There are no *in between* scores.

Defects	If this defect is clearly visible in your enterprise, score these marks	Your score
Management		
1. Autocratic boss who dominates his colleagues and takes no advice from them.	8	
2. The boss is also the chairman.	4	
3. Passive board of management not actively participating in decisions.	2	
4. Skills on the board are unbalanced, eg there are too many engineers	2	
5. No competent, strong-minded finance man guiding the business.	2	
6. Where relevant, no depth of management below the board.	1	
Accounting		
1. No budget (If there is, it is not compared with actual each month.)	3	
2. No cash flow plan (If there is, it is out of date.)	3	
3. No costing system: no one knows what each product really costs, nor its cash contribution to overheads.	3	
Response to change		
The enterprise exhibits some clear and vital example of failing to respond to change, eg: — An ageing product — Old-fashioned plant — Out-of-date marketing — Outmoded attitude to employees — Ageing management — No computer	15	
TOTAL FOR DEFECTS	43	

Mistakes	If this mistake is clearly visible in your enterprise, score these marks	Your score
Leverage The *capital gearing* (external borrowing: proprietor's funds), *or* The *income gearing* (profit before interest and tax: interest) of the enterprise is noticeably high.	15	
Overtrading Turnover is rising at a much faster rate than the finance available to fund it.	15	
Projects The enterprise has launched a project (eg building a factory, launching a new major product, guaranteeing a subsidiary company's loan) of such a size that if it goes wrong it will bring down the enterprise.	15	
TOTAL FOR MISTAKES	45	

Symptom of failure	*If this sympton of failure is clearly visible in your enterprise, score these marks*	*Your score*
Financial signs Control ratios are deteriorating and cash is becoming extremely scarce.	4	
Creative accounting Accounts show evidence of window dressing to 'improve' profits, eg stocks valued higher, depreciation lower, repairs capitalised etc.	4	
Non-financial signs of distress Examples: Office needs painting, top management salaries frozen, capital expenditure decisions delayed, product quality or service deteriorating, morale failing.	3	
Nose-dive Impossible to hide the last-gasp scramble for survival: writs, rumours, resignations.	1	
TOTAL FOR SYMPTOMS OF FAILURE	12	
GRAND TOTAL	100	

Is your score 25 or above?

If so, there are grounds for serious concern about the future of your business. *Now* is the time to get additional help from your accountant, bank manager, the Small Firms Service, or your Local Enterprise Agency.

Profit improvement

The break-even chart on page 62 helps us to understand the *five* basic ways of improving profitability:

Key
Dotted line = projected figures
Unbroken line = current figures

1. *Increase selling prices*

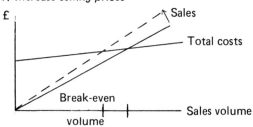

Increase prices with nil or acceptable decrease in sales volume to reduce the break-even volume — but see page 39.

2. *Reduce variable costs*

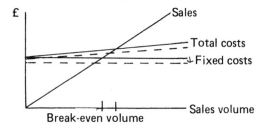

Reduce direct materials and/or direct labour costs to reduce variable costs. Thus total costs fall and reduce the break-even volume — see page 95.

3. *Reduce overheads (fixed costs)*

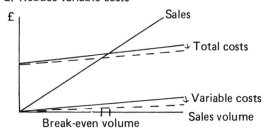

Reduce overheads to reduce total costs, in turn reducing the break-even volume — see page 96.

4. *Increase sales volume*

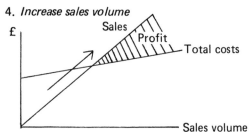

Move up the sales line by selling more without disturbing selling prices, fixed or variable costs. All sales above break-even volume yield a profit. Therefore, the higher the volume, the higher the profit if all the other items remain constant — see pages 46-52).

5. *Improve product mix*

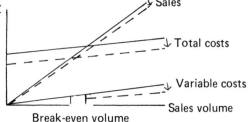

Concentrate on more profitable lines — often selling less in total — but also making correspondingly greater reductions in variable costs to reduce the break-even volume (see pages 39 and 62).

These are the only ways of increasing profitability

The end

The biggest losses are incurred by *'pouring good money after bad'*.

Sometimes the financial problem is one of cash where creditors cannot be paid, though asset values exceed all liabilities. Where the business is simply not paying its way early action is important to avoid debts running higher than necessary. Creditors will often wait for asset sales if they are kept informed of plans and progress by the proprietor. Full communication with creditors is essential.

Limited company

At the very end, there are just a small number of *options*:

Type of liquidation	Instigated by	Requirements	Method
1. Voluntary	Resolution of 75 per cent of members	Still solvent	Liquidator appointed by members
	Resolution of members	Insolvent	Creditors' meeting Liquidator appointed by creditors
2. Imposed by the court	Creditor	Mainly cannot pay debts	Court appoints liquidator, often Official Receiver
	Member	Disputes between members	
3. Under court supervision	Plaintiff	Evidence of fraud or corruption in winding up	Application to the court

Where business failure looks increasingly likely, professional advice should be taken sufficiently early to safeguard the option for a members' voluntary liquidation (1 above).

The usual order of distribution of assets by the liquidator will be:

1. Debts secured by a fixed charge
2. Winding-up expenses
3. Preferential debtors, including:
   - rates
   - UK taxes (contact your accountant)
   - four months' wages and salaries to a limit of £800 per annum
   - accrued holiday remuneration
   - contributions payable under Social Security Acts
   - PAYE deductions
4. Debts secured by a floating charge
5. Unsecured creditors
6. Deferred creditors
7. Shareholders

Partnership

Type of liquidation	Instigated by	Requirements	Method
1. Voluntary	One or more of the partners	Parting of the ways, change of interests, retirement etc	1. By agreement of partners 2. By notice by one partner to the others 3. By any method laid down in the partnership agreement (if any)
2. Forced	Usually a creditor	Insolvency	Court proceedings for recovery of money followed by a court judgment and then appointment of a receiver. And/or bankruptcy proceedings against one or more of the partners when personal assets in addition to business assets may be vulnerable
3. Selling the business	Partners	From choice, eg retirement, change of interests etc	Usually by sale of the business as a 'going concern' often including goodwill value

Partners are usually each responsible for *all* liabilities of the partnership so far as creditors are concerned. Internal sharing agreements do not affect this principle. Partnerships are best regulated by written agreement; otherwise the Partnership Act 1890 applies and some of the provisions are antiquated.

Sole trader

Type of liquidation	Instigated by	Requirements	Method
1. Voluntary	Proprietor	Cessation, eg retirement	Payment of liabilities, collection of debts owed to the business, sale of assets if appropriate. Accountant's advice usually required regarding taxation and other fiscal points arising
2. Forced	Usually a creditor, otherwise by the proprietor on realisation of insolvency	Insolvency, ie total liabilities exceed total assets	Legal proceedings, sometimes resulting in bankruptcy or Administration Order, ie payment of debts through the court
3. Selling the business	Proprietor	From choice, eg retirement, change of interests etc	Usually by sale of the business as a 'going concern' often including goodwill value

Further Reading

Chapter 1

Creating Your Own Work, M Mason (Gresham Books)
Starting a Successful Small Business, M J Morris (Kogan Page)
Working for Yourself, Godfrey Golzen (Kogan Page)

Chapter 2

Buying a Shop, A St J Price (Kogan Page)
The Guardian Guide to Running a Small Business, Clive Woodcock
   (Kogan Page)
How to Buy a Business, Peter Farrell (Kogan Page)
Just for Starters, A Bollard (Intermediate Technology)
Small Beginnings, A Bollard (Intermediate Technology)
The Small Business Guide, Colin Barrow (BBC Publications)
Starting a Small Business, D Fowler (Sphere)
Taking up a Franchise, G Golzen and C Barrow (Kogan Page)
Running Your Own Cooperative, John Pearce (Kogan Page)
Work for Yourself, P Hall (National Extension College)

Chapter 3

Choosing and Using Professional Advisers, P Chaplin (Kogan Page)

Chapter 4

Effective Advertising, H C Carter (Kogan Page)
Effective Marketing for the Smaller Business, G Lace (Scope Books)
Getting Sales, Richard D Smith and Ginger Dick (Kogan Page)
How to Win Profitable Business, T Cannon (Hutchinson)
Managing a Sales Force, M Wilson (Gower Press)
Successful Marketing for the Small Business, Dave Patten (Kogan Page)

Chapter 5

Financial Management for the Small Business, Colin Barrow
   (Kogan Page)
Financing for Small Business, K Checkley (Sphere)
Money for Business, Bank of England
Raising Finance: The Guardian Guide for Small Business,
   Clive Woodcock (Kogan Page)

Chapter 6

Planning Permission — A Guide for Industry, HMSO

Chapter 7

Law for the Small Business, Patricia Clayton (Kogan Page)

Chapter 8

Make a Success of Micro Computing in Your Business, Parnell, Jackson
   & Lucas (Enterprise Books)
Simplified Book-keeping for Small Businesses, G Whitehead (Vyner)
Understand Your Accounts, A St J Price (Kogan Page)

Chapter 9

The Daily Telegraph Recruitment Handbook, Penny Hackett, Philip
   Schofield & Michael Armstrong (Kogan Page)
A Handbook of Personnel Management Practice, Michael Armstrong
   (Kogan Page)

Chapter 10

Help for Growing Business, Department of Trade and Industry
Successful Expansion for the Small Business, M J Morris (Kogan Page)

Titles related to specific businesses

The Kelvin Handbook of Optical Practice Development, P A Management
   Consultants
Running Your Own Antiques Business, Noël Riley & Godfrey Golzen
   (Kogan Page)
Running Your Own Boarding Kennels, Sheila Zabawa (Kogan Page)
Running Your Own Building Business, Kim Ludman (Kogan Page)
Running Your Own Catering Business, Ursula Garner & Judy Ridgway
   (Kogan Page)
Running Your Own Driving School, Nigel Stacey (Kogan Page)
Running Your Own Hairdressing Salon, Christine Harvey & Helen
   Steadman (Kogan Page)
Running Your Own Photographic Business, John Rose & Linda Hankin
   (Kogan Page)
Running Your Own Pub, Elven Money (Kogan Page)
Running Your Own Restaurant, Diane Hughes & Godfrey Golzen
   (Kogan Page)
Running Your Own Shop, Roger Cox (Kogan Page)
Running Your Own Small Hotel, Joy Lennick (Kogan Page)
Running Your Own Wine Bar, Judy Ridgway (Kogan Page)

Index